Dear Grandma: Your Grandkids Are Unschoolers

Sheila Baranoski

To Alisha: I wouldn't be a grandma without you.
Thank you for being the wonderful daughter that you are,
and thank you for being the wonderful parent that you are.
I love you.

**Other Books by
Sheila Baranoski:**

Cellular Spirits

Miss Crazy

Introduction

If you're concerned about someone you love who is an unschooler, this book is for you. I'm going to use the word grandma because it's easier to say than grandma, grandpa, aunt, uncle, sister, brother, or anyone else who is concerned.

Unschooling. Your adult kids are at it again, making life choices and parenting choices that you would never make, that you don't understand, or that go against the grain. While I'm an unschooling mother of three, I'm also a grandmother. My daughter is also an unschooling parent, but doesn't always do things the way I did, and that's a good thing. It's a whole different ball game, loving those two grandkids more than I can say but not having the final say on everything they do.

Maybe you simply want to understand what un-schooling is. Maybe you want to understand why your grandchildren's parents interact with the kids the way they do (or why they don't want you to interact with them in certain ways). Maybe there's been some tension over unschooling. My hope is that this book will help by explaining what unschooling is all about and by giving some reasons they might have chosen it. I'm not your daughter, and you're not my parent. It's not personal for us, so we can keep this purely philosophical.

Throughout the book, I'm going to answer questions you might have, such as how they'll learn everything they need to know, how they'll support themselves, why the rules are so different in their family, and what about socialization, discipline, and college? You'll hear stories of how my own unschooled children and grandchildren learn. My daughter Alisha is an adult with children of her own. Her son Tripp is five, and her son Storm is three. My son Matt is nineteen, and my son Luke is seventeen.

Some unschoolers, when trying to keep peace with the grandparents, don't explain exactly what unschooling is. They give just little bits and pieces because they worry that you won't accept or understand how unschooling works. I'm not going to do that to you. I'm going to share the straight-up facts, grandparent to grandparent. Some of it might be so different from what you're used to that it might seem shocking or upsetting at first. It takes some getting used to, so I urge you to not stop reading the first time I hit you with something that sounds crazy. It makes sense the longer you think about it.

I have talked to grandparents who were upset that their kids were unschooling because they assumed that their kids chose this lifestyle because they didn't think their own upbringing was good enough. Let me assure you, Grandma. It's not about you. Sometimes adult children simply choose different philosophies. Even if they think their philosophy is better than the philosophy you believed in that doesn't mean that they think they're better than you or that they don't love and respect you. As a matter of fact, the entire last chapter of the book is about how important grandparents are and how their involvement is beneficial.

Chapter One

What Unschooling Is (and Isn't)

You might have heard the words homeschooling and unschooling used interchangeably, but unschoolers operate from a different philosophy than the kind of homeschooling that uses curriculum. It's sometimes just easier for unschoolers to call themselves homeschoolers because more people are familiar with homeschooling. Also, unschoolers must legally follow their state's homeschool law.

Homeschooling is legal in all fifty states. I won't get into the legal requirements of homeschooling since they vary from state to state (and country to country).

While homeschoolers must comply with their state's homeschool law, they have the freedom to learn in whatever way seems best to them. Some homeschool parents buy textbooks and set up their home just like a school, complete with chalk boards and recess breaks. Some choose hands-on projects and field trips instead of textbooks. Some use a mixture of formal curriculum and hands-on projects. Whatever their style, homeschooling parents generally decide what and how their children learn, with varying degrees of input from their children.

In unschooling families, however, it's the children who decide what and how they learn. Parents guide and support them but don't dictate a curriculum. In practice, their lives look a lot different than the lives of traditional homeschoolers.

The meaning of unschooling is right in the word itself. The prefix un- means "not." We all know what schooling means. So un-schooling means not schooling. It's not unlearning, it's learning without school.

It has been debated about what to call this type of learning. Some people think the word unschooling sounds too negative, focusing on what isn't happening instead of on the learning that is happening. Some people call it life learning or natural learning. But the word unschooling has stuck, and it's the word most people use.

The word unschooling was first used in the 1970s by a teacher, author, and school reform advocate named John Holt. He was interested in studying how children learn, and spent a lot of time writing about how schools could improve the learning experience for children. He eventually came to the conclusion that schools didn't want, or perhaps in some cases, were not able to change. So he encouraged parents to allow their children to learn at home. Some of his later books were *Teach Your Own* and *Instead of Education*. If you're interested in reading educational philosophy, his ideas are fabulous.

He was inspired by the signs for "uncola." We all know that 7-Up® and Sprite® are still soft drinks. But they're not cola.

Unschooling is like that. It's learning, but it's most definitely not school. People often use this quote from John Holt's book *How Children Learn* to explain unschooling.

"Birds fly, fish swim, man thinks and learns. Therefore, we do not need to motivate children into learning by wheedling, bribing or bullying. We do not need to keep picking away at their minds to make sure they are learning. What we need to do, and all we need to do, is bring as much of the world as we can into the school and classroom (in our case, into their lives); give children as much help and guidance as they ask for; listen respectfully when they feel like talking; and then get out of the way. We can trust them to do the rest."

Unschoolers live their lives as if school doesn't exist, trusting that learning is a natural process for humans. It's as natural for us to learn as it is for us to breathe.

This isn't lazy parenting. Just as we make sure our kids are in an environment with clean air so they can breathe well, unschooling parents put a lot of effort into creating an environment where kids can learn well. It isn't ignoring the kids and letting them fend for themselves. We make sure they have the materials, resources, time, and freedom they need. Sometimes that means driving them somewhere. Sometimes that means giving them the space at home to do their own thing. Sometimes it means finding them a mentor, a club, or a class that seems to be a perfect fit for what they want to know. Sometimes it means providing the materials they need for a project. It always means trusting the child and the human drive to learn.

Children learn what they need, when they need it, without being forced. Unschoolers don't make their kids use textbooks, worksheets, or curriculum. We don't make them write an essay about a field trip they took. We don't even make them go on a field trip if they don't want to go. We don't make them choose a book to read. We don't make them watch an "educational" game or TV show over a "noneducational" game or show. We don't ask them to choose what they're going to learn for science this year. In the real world, we don't divide life into subjects, so we don't do that as unschoolers either. It may be shocking to some to hear all the things that unschoolers don't do, but keep reading and you'll see all that we do.

We give them a life that is full and rich with things they're interested in and passionate about. Everything is educational, and there's learning in everything. There's no dichotomy between their play and their learning. It's all intertwined.

Following a child's lead can push parents (and grandparents!) out of their comfort zones. Introvert parents might find themselves going to lots of social activities; extrovert parents might find themselves staying home more often than they'd choose. A mom who hates technology might find herself helping a child build a website, and a mom with no love for the outdoors might find herself putting a worm on a fishhook.

Unschooling is about what's best for the individual child, not what's easiest or most convenient for the adults.

And then there's radical unschooling.

Radical unschooling, sometimes called whole life unschooling, and sometimes called just plain old unschooling, takes it a step further. Just as we trust our children with their learning, we trust them in other areas as well: like when to go to bed and when to wake up, what to eat, what to wear, what to read, what music to listen to, what to watch on TV, and how many video games they play. Essentially, they choose the setting where their learning takes place and the materials they will learn from. I'll cover radical unschooling in depth later on in the book. Not all unschoolers are radical unschoolers, and some embrace certain aspects of radical unschooling while rejecting others.

There are so many little differences between families that there's a chance that not everything I cover in this book will apply to your family. Take what applies and leave what doesn't.

Learning is everywhere, but if children are to learn what's right for them, they must choose the path that will be best for them to learn that. Radical unschooling allows them to choose their own path by deciding for themselves the what, where, when, and how they do everything. No curriculum or teacher can know what untapped talents and passions are hidden inside a child. Their intuition, a prompting that comes from deep inside themselves, will lead them to explore exactly what they need in order to develop themselves so they can do what they're uniquely meant to do with their lives.

Unschoolers trust children. Because we trust them, we have a consensual partnership relationship with our children rather than an authoritarian one. We strive to set an example for our children, but we don't lord authority over them. We've lived on this earth longer than they have, so we often have valuable insights to share with them, but our leadership is a natural role, not one we force and demand. I know that goes against what mainstream society says we should do with children. Keep reading and I'll explain more. I hope I'll be able to set your mind at ease.

Chapter Two

Times Are Changing

Things have changed since John Holt wrote about learning and unschooling in the 1960s and 1970s. Today, the philosophy of unschooling is even more relevant. We no longer live in the Industrial Age, which relied heavily on physical labor to run machines, or even the Information Age, which relied heavily on logical, analytical skills to run computers.

Seth Godin is a prolific author who talks about how our economy has shifted to what he calls the connection economy, where we can connect to other people easily through the Internet. In his 2012 book *The Icarus Deception: How High Will You Fly?*, he tells the story of cruft. "Cruft," he explains, "is the engineering term for the leftover detritus, useless computer code, broken devices, empty boxes, and junk that we have to maneuver around as technology advances." He tells of Cruft Lab in Harvard. "Over the decades, abandoned radar components, obsolete circuit boards, and outdated vacuum tubes began to pile up in the lab. The windows were stacked full of cruft, things that used to be important but were now simply in the way."

Then he goes on to say this, and as I read it, all I could think about was school. School is cruft. "The Industrial Age, the one that established our schooling, our workday, our economy, and our expectations, is dying. It's dying faster than most of us expected, and it's causing plenty of pain, indecision, and fear as it goes.

"We're surrounded by the cruft of the Industrial Age. By the expectations, beliefs, and standards of an era that's now over.

"What an opportunity, to be among the first to clean it out, to ignore it, to move to a different building altogether. A life without cruft slowing you down. A career focusing on what you can create instead of what you must replicate."

Unschoolers already do what Godin advocates: Come up with their own ideas rather than replicate someone else's. Unschooled kids do grow up able to support themselves with work that is meaningful to them (more on that in Chapter Eight). But they do not receive an assembly line education and aren't trained to work an assembly line job.

American schools were modeled after the Prussian education system, which was designed to create obedient citizens and soldiers, as well as good consumers and factory workers for the Industrial Age. They trained kids to respond to bells in order to move from one task to the next, the way they would if they worked in a factory. They trained kids to not complain about boredom, to do what they're told in the way they're told to do it. Producing what the factory schools wanted them to produce, to the standards the schools wanted it produced, was more important when training kids to succeed in the mainstream Industrial Age economy. Now, more than ever, we can encourage kids to listen to themselves and march to the beat of their own drums.

Schools say kids should act extremely interested in whatever topic the teacher brings up—and they'll be rewarded with a good grade based on how eagerly they participate. However, they should only be extremely interested in that topic until the bell rings, when they move to the next spot on the assembly line. They should quickly switch gears then be extremely interested in whatever the next teacher presents to them. Instead of admonishing children to listen to their teachers, perhaps we should be admonishing ourselves to listen to our children. We often blame television and corporations, or even an assumed greedy nature of children, for children wanting all the popular toys and gadgets. Perhaps children wouldn't be so easily influenced by commercials if schools hadn't trained them that good kids want what they're told to want.

If your grandchildren are unschoolers, especially if they've been raised with the unschooling philosophy from birth, you might find that they are, in some ways, different from other kids. They might be less compliant, less likely to obey orders. Less predictable, less standardized. They might not know all the facts that other kids their age seem to know because they learn on a different schedule unique to themselves. But look more deeply at the individuals they are. You'll find skills, talents, and knowledge about things that aren't the products of industrialized schooling. Get to know them well enough to know their thoughts on literature, social justice, and politics. Their opinions and reasoning might differ from yours, but they're likely very interesting. Listen with fascination as they explain to you why the campfire crackles, facts about dinosaurs, or the biography of their favorite video game developer.

When one of my sons was little, he pointed out that Santa and the other reindeer, who are supposed to be jolly and loving, didn't want anything to do with Rudolph until they saw how his difference was useful to them. Rudolph's parents tried to cover up his shiny red nose so that he would fit in and do well in reindeer school, but his uniqueness shone through anyway. I don't want to be like Rudolph's parents, trying to squeeze my children or grandchildren into society's mold. I want to celebrate their uniqueness and let it shine.

Some argue that kids need school so they can do well on the SAT and get into college. In Chapter Eight, I discuss more about how unschoolers can get into college. While unschooling certainly doesn't keep a kid from doing well on the SAT if that's his goal (and unschoolers can impress college admissions officers without years of schooling), those kinds of test-taking skills will start to matter less and less. Many colleges now make such tests optional because they realize that the SAT was created to measure an education received from schools training kids to be obedient and compliant, not innovative and creative. A September 25, 2015, *Washington Post* blog post reported that Hampshire College is refusing to even look at SAT or ACT scores. In the post, Hampshire's President Jonathan Lash said, "If we reduce education to the outcomes of a test, the only incentive for schools and students to innovate is in the form of improving test-taking and scores. Teaching to a test becomes stifling for teachers and students, far from the inspiring, adaptive education which most benefits students. Our greatly accelerating world needs graduates who are trained to address tough situations with innovation, ingenuity, entrepreneurship and a capacity for mobilizing collaboration and cooperation."

www.washingtonpost.com/blogs/answer-sheet/wp/2015/09/25/what-one-college-discovered-when-it-stopped-accepting-satact-scores/?postshare=8941443453939626

Some elementary and high schools are slowly changing their methods, trying to catch up. But the problem is that in order to make themselves perfect places for kids to learn and grow to be all they can be in this new world, they would have to make themselves look more like unschoolers. They can take giving kids freedom and celebrating individuality only so far, because an institution is, by its very nature, not very good at honoring individuality. As long as school is compulsory, and there are punishments and rewards just for attendance, let alone performing to certain standards, they will always fall short in preparing kids for the real world.

In his book *Teach Your Own*, John Holt said, "What is most important and valuable about the home as a base for children's growth into the world is not that it is a better school than the schools, but that it isn't a school at all."

Schools are based on a model that simply doesn't fit the world anymore. But outside of school, children can do whatever helps them thrive individually.

No one needs to be forced to attend school in order to follow the path they were meant to follow, whether they're artists and dreamers or number crunchers and data analyzers. We need to throw all the molds away and, instead of making children be our students, become students of our children.

Chapter Three

Academics

I'm sure you and your unschooled family will agree that learning is extremely important. Most unschooling parents have spent significant time learning about learning. Unschooling theory isn't mainstream, but it's definitely rooted in some solid principles of how people learn.

Intellectual Skills Versus Academic Skills

When I was in high school back in the '80s, before I or anyone I knew had ever used the Internet, I took a computer class. I left that class believing that I hated computers. I've since learned that I love computers. I use them for writing, paying bills, keeping records, communicating with people all over the world, shopping—you name it. I'd have a hard time going a day without one.

Everything I use my computer for, I learned without school. Most things I learned by messing around on my own. However, for some things I asked people more knowledgeable for help in learning (usually my teenage sons, who have never been to school).

My teens have learned basic html and coding through Minecraft®. When I wanted to start using Drop Box® for business, they already knew how to do it because they use it for their own projects. When I needed to send pictures to someone in a zipped file, once again I looked to my teens.

When I asked my son how he knew how to unzip a file, he said, "Um, I've been using a computer all my life. How do you not know?"

Peter Gray, PhD, is a Harvard Researcher who studies education from a biological perspective. In his article "How Early Academics Retards Intellectual Development,"

www.psychologytoday.com/blog/freedom-learn/201506/how-early-academic-training-retards-intellectual-development,

he talks about the difference between intellectual skills and academic skills. He describes intellectual skills as "a person's ways of reasoning, hypothesizing, exploring, understanding, and in general, making sense of the world." In other words, what we do when we're playing and pondering. He describes academic skills as "...tried and true means of organizing, manipulating, or responding to specific categories of information to achieve certain ends." Or all those things that schools force on kids with drill and rote memorization.

Unschooling's strength is that it fosters strong intellectual skills. We don't drill our kids to learn the ABCs. We don't make them memorize times tables.

They aren't tested to see if they know the state capitals. It might look like they do nothing but play all the time, but what they're doing by playing is developing background concepts of things they're interested in so that their intellectual skills are strong. The academic things that they would be forced to memorize if they went to school aren't nearly as helpful to long-term learning without strong intellectual skills developed through play and meaningful life experiences. When they need to learn one of those academic skills, they can apply themselves and learn them quickly.

It's why my teens, who were brought up immersed in a world of technology, can understand how to use a spreadsheet in minutes while their mom still struggles. They had plenty of time to "just play around" on computers. I didn't get on the Internet until my middle child was a baby. When I was a teenager in the '80s, the Atari 2600 was new, and Pac-Man® was the most complicated video game I played. Taking an academic computer class in high school didn't do anything for me because I'd never had the luxury of developing intellectual skills by growing up with plenty of free computer play.

We can apply the intellectual versus academic skills in every subject.

Reading

Reading is a big concern that grandparents often have. Unschoolers aren't drilled on the alphabet or phonics or expected to remember words from a reading list. So how do they learn to read?

Not all kids learn to read in the same way or at the same age. My daughter read at age four, and my boys both read at age eleven.

How children learn to read without schooling is as hard to explain as how children learn to walk without lessons. They just do. It's a natural thing for humans to learn to communicate with other humans in the way that they see them communicating.

One evening I was hanging out with my grandkids, and my daughter had gone downstairs to get something. We needed tape to hang something on the wall, so I suggested that we text her. I helped the four-year-old hit the correct letters on my phone.

"Will you bring tape up with you?"

Simple interactions like this let kids know that this is how our society communicates and that there's a real reason to use words in order to communicate with the people around them.

While I can't explain the inner functioning of the brain that helps us learn to read naturally, I can give you the stories of how my children learn. My kids aren't smarter than most kids, able to pick something up that most kids need lessons to learn. They aren't exceptions to a rule. This is what it looks like when reading unfolds naturally. Other unschooling parents have different stories, and while their stories may be different, the end results are all the same: kids who read.

How Matt Learned to Read

It's a leap of faith to trust natural learning when so many around you don't understand unschooling. When Matt was six, people said, "He'll pick it up soon," probably because they assumed I spent every day drilling phonics. When he was seven, they started to raise eyebrows. At eight and nine? "That child should be reading!" At ten or eleven? People didn't know what to say. Matt learned to read not long after his eleventh birthday. Most kids naturally learn to read before they're twelve, but some do learn later than twelve, and I'm sure those parents get a lot of negative comments.

Matt didn't care what people thought. He didn't even give it any consideration. He played happily through his entire childhood because he was free and respected.

I don't think most people mean to be disrespectful of unschoolers' choices. I just think the idea that a child won't learn unless he's taught is so ingrained in our society that people can't imagine any other way. So is the idea that learning is hard and kids avoid it unless they're made to do it. After all, if children don't need to be drilled in order to learn even basic stuff like reading, why do we send our kids to school? Why do we punish or reward them for report card grades? When they ask why they have to go to school, why do we tell them it's because they won't learn if they don't go? Why, indeed.

I knew in my heart I should trust. I still heard voices of doubt from time to time. What if I'm ruining my child and he never learns to read, and one day he's an illiterate adult asking me, "Why did you do this to me? Why didn't you make me learn to read?" But although I had the occasional panic, I never acted on it. I silenced it, listened to my heart, and trusted Matt's natural learning process to unfold.

He went through a period of frustration. "I want to know how to read now." So I offered to give him reading lessons. We tried the lessons, several different times using different approaches, but after a few days, he told me that he just couldn't take those lessons anymore, so we stopped. Looking back, I realize he was going through a mental growth spurt that was uncomfortable for him, and his "I want to know how to read now" was a voicing of the discomfort of his growth spurt instead of a need for lessons. When a boy is anxious to grow his first beard, we don't teach him hair-growing strategies. We just tell him to be patient, puberty will come. I assured him that he would learn to read when he was ready, that I understood that he was frustrated, and I would read anything to him that he wanted.

His frustration caused me another brief period of doubt. He was frustrated, and maybe he wouldn't be if he had learned to read in the traditional way. But then I stopped and calmed myself. I had offered him the traditional reading lessons, he tried them, and he declined to continue them. He would learn to read when he was ready. Trust, trust, trust.

Then he started complaining that there are words EVERYWHERE and that he hates it. "Why does this house have so many WORDS in it? They're all over the place!" He picked up a sale paper that had fallen off the dining room table. "They're even under the table!" He ran to his room, and I heard him saying, "They're up here, too!"

He said, "I don't WANT to read them, but they're always right there in front of me, and I just have to try to figure them out."

Not long before his eleventh birthday, we were in the car and the kids were getting bored, so I suggested the alphabet game. You know, the one where you find a sign outside of the car that has a letter of the alphabet. You have to do one letter at a time, in alphabetical order, and you can't skip ahead. Even though Qs are very hard to find, you can't count any Qs you find until you've found a P.

We were looking for the letter F, and he said, "Does slow have an F in it?"

I said, "Why?"

He said, "Because that sign back there said 'slow,' and I was wondering if it had an F." Somehow he had recognized "slow" but not the letters in it. He was certainly not figuring out reading by any method I would have dreamed up to teach him. I was surprised that he was able to read the word "slow." As far as I knew, he only knew a small selection of words: Lego®. Star Wars®. Save. Continue. (See the video game theme?) Mom. Dad.

Every once in a while, he would pick out one word on a page and read it. I'd get excited and think, "Any day now!"

If I had to make predictions about the first sentence he would read, I wouldn't have guessed it would be from a fortune cookie. But that's how things go with natural learning. Our world is our museum, and when your "reading curriculum" is everything you come into contact with in the world, you just never know what will happen.

I had taken his brother Luke out to eat because he had watched something about sushi on the Disney Channel and wanted to try some. Matt hadn't wanted to go with us, so I brought home a fortune cookie for him. He opened it, looked at the paper, and read it. "Don't put all your eggs in one basket." And he went about his business as though he had not just done something exciting. Well, he might not have been excited, but I sure was!

So I thought, now it will be any day, and he'll be like one of those miracle unschooled children who had never read a book in their lives then one day picked up *The Lord of the Rings* and read it from beginning to end in one sitting. (Yes, it does happen, but it's not typical.) I laid books all over the place that I thought might interest him, but never saw him pick them up. Although he had loved when I read the *Harry Potter and His Dark Materials* series to him, he often declined to join Luke and me when I read other books out loud. "I'm just not a big book person," he'd say.

I turned the dial on my panic to Off and trusted.

We went to the fair, and he said, "Why do all the drink stands say ice cold drinks? I never knew they said that! Why would they have to say that? Doesn't everyone assume that the drinks they buy will be cold?" The fair was a different experience for him that year. And, unlike the frustration he felt several months before at the words on the sale paper on our dining room floor, he was now interested.

I never pressured him. I never did the "Can you tell me what this says?" type of quizzing. When he asked me what something said, I never said, "Why don't you try to figure it out yourself?" I knew he wanted to figure it out for himself, and that pushing him would only frustrate him.

Sometimes I'd see him looking at a video game guide, studying it for a long period of time, not coming to ask me to read it to him like he always used to. Then one day he came to me holding a guide book, and once again, asked, "Will you read this to me? I just don't feel like reading these paragraphs. They're too long."

And so I did. I didn't push him to keep trying when he asked me to read to him. He knew how to push himself when he was ready to be pushed and ask for help when he needed it. My job as an unschooling parent was to trust the natural learning process and respect my child.

Finally, my son read his first book. Not Charles Dickens or Shakespeare, but not Dick and Jane either. He skipped Dick and Jane and moved right to *The Little Book of Knock-Knock Jokes*. It contains words like pencil, mountain, cantaloupe, and orangutan. I don't know how the boys and I got into telling knock-knock jokes, but after I read lots of jokes from lots of websites and spent lots of time listening to little boys giggling over made-up jokes, I remembered a cute little book that my aunt had mailed the kids, and had been on our shelves for over a year waiting to be loved. I said, "You might like this book. It's all knock-knock jokes." I left it sitting out. The next afternoon, he was reading it.

Now maybe I should count the video game guide books as his first books, but he never read them out loud to me. I never knew for sure how much he was reading at a time, how well he was reading them, or how much he was understanding. But I knew he was reading the knock-knock jokes well because he read those he liked to me and rejected the ones he didn't. I know he comprehended because he laughed at the jokes.

We got the video game *Animal Crossing* for the Wii console game system for Christmas, and I overheard him reading parts of it to Luke. I remembered all the times I'd read an earlier version of *Animal Crossing* on the GameCube® console system to Matt, patiently trusting that he would one day do it on his own. It made me smile to hear him reading the more modern version of the game to his brother.

Why is it so hard for humans to trust? Why do we need to come up with detailed plans and try to control and measure every step?

I was fascinated to watch Matt's reading unfold. There were times when I would have loved to look inside his mind to see what he was thinking about, to prove to myself that he was learning. But part of the learning process is meant to be private. It's a sacred thing to grow into our own person. I couldn't see all the things that went on inside Matt's head as he learned to read any more than I could see the hormones that later grew his beard. But I could trust and watch in awe and wonder.

Luke followed a similar path. His reading began soon before his twelfth birthday. It was easier to trust his learning process to unfold because Matt had shown me how.

Matt is nineteen now, and you would never be able to tell whether he began reading at four or eleven. If you have a grandchild who isn't reading yet, relax. I know you don't want him to be "behind," but unschooling works differently.

In school, if you don't follow the progression of academic skills in the way they present them to you, you'll be behind what your classmates are doing. You'll be put in the slow classes, and you'll be considered dumb by teachers and other students. Don't think kids don't know that kids are often grouped together based on how smart the teacher has judged them to be, and that can lead them to form an opinion of their own intelligence that can stay with them for the rest of their lives. But with unschoolers, the intellectual skills are built up so strongly that you'll not be able to tell which adult was reading at four and which didn't read until fourteen, or any other age in between those two extremes.

A teacher friend of mine told me that natural learning was not what he was taught about reading in college. Of course it's not. School works on the belief that without someone telling a kid what to learn, when to learn it, how to learn it, and adding some rewards (gold stars, grades, and honor rolls) or punishment (You'll have to write those words ten times if you spell them wrong!), kids won't learn. That belief system has a very low opinion of natural human inquisitiveness and ability to learn. In our society, a child in a normal, healthy environment is surrounded by people communicating with the written word and will inevitably learn to read.

Unschooler after unschooler has proven that if you live in an environment where people are reading, writing, and having interesting conversations, learning to read happens naturally.

Writing

I'm a writer, so all aspects of writing are important to me. But as important as it is to me, I don't think kids need to be made to sit in a classroom with a textbook to learn it. All language skills begin with the everyday conversation kids hear around them.

Kids tend to speak the same way their parents do, whether they go to school or not. If you want kids to use proper grammar, be very, very careful to set a good example. If you don't use proper grammar, making them endure grammar lessons is probably not going to change much.

The same is true for vocabulary. If kids hear a wide range of interesting words, they'll use a wide range of interesting words. Looking up lists of words in the dictionary and writing their meaning five times isn't what makes for a good vocabulary.

None of my kids have ever had grammar or vocabulary lessons, homework, or tests. I read to them a lot, for as long as they were interested in being read to. We listened to audio books on car trips. We made up stories together. We discussed video game plots and news stories. We did lots and lots and lots of discussing. My kids speak the way my husband and I speak.

Researchers from the University of Kansas did a famous study called "The Thirty Million Word Gap." Their study showed that low-income children hear thirty million less words by the age of three, and that this greatly impacts their future success. One thing that unschoolers of any income bracket never need to worry about is the thirty million word gap. Unschooled kids get experiences perfectly suited to their individual personalities and interests, and plenty of experiences lead to plenty of conversations. Reading is very important, and we do read a lot to our kids and give them many opportunities to be around the written word. But books aren't the only way to develop a large vocabulary. Someone asked me once how my son, who was a "late reader" by school standards (but right on time by his own individual schedule), had such a great vocabulary even before he was reading on his own. The answer is simple. I read to him a lot, but I also talked to him a lot. We pondered how to rig something up to fix the drip that the air conditioner was making, talked about the latest news from the Nintendo® world, and discussed details about trips we wanted to take. Unschooling families do things together, and kids are welcome to join the adults doing real work in the real world. Real world experiences that are meaningful for children help them retain vocabulary better than boring lectures they have no choice but to attend, and dry textbooks that someone else has chosen for them and forced them to read.

Several universities are working with lower income families to help them do what unschoolers already do: talk to their kids more. While "The Thirty Million Word Gap" study was aimed at kids three and under, I believe the values that these universities promote—talking to your kids more about lots of interesting things and ideas—are just as important for older kids and teens. Author Frank Smith, in *The Book of Learning and Forgetting*, talks about studies that show how many new words children learn per day and per year. As I read the studies he cited in his book, I wasn't surprised to read that very young children learn new words at a very high rate since they aren't born talking. By age six, children have a vocabulary of about ten thousand words. One study claimed that infants learn one new word for every hour they're awake. But what I found amazing to read was that this crazy rate of learning continues. Between third and fourth grade, a child learns an average of twenty-seven words a day. And it doesn't stop there! Teenagers are still learning an average of ten words a day. Of course, average means that some are learning many less and some are learning many more. These studies aren't talking about words learned for a test and then forgotten. These are words that become a permanent part of their vocabulary, most of which he tells us are probably not learned through schoolwork.

Unschoolers don't sit their kids down and force them to learn what a noun is; they create a rich foundation of intellectual skills gained by just enjoying language. If they ever want to play Mad Libs® and need to know what a noun is, they can figure it out pretty quickly.

I was in my thirties when I discovered my passion for writing. Since then I've spent years playing with words and ideas, going to writers' workshops and critique groups, and reading blogs and books about writing. Before my *Cellular Spirits* series, I wrote another full-length novel that wasn't good enough to publish, but it was important that I had spent time writing it for the joy of writing. Writing that subpar beginner's novel was the development of intellectual skills that Peter Gray talked about. If my editor sends me an explanation of proper punctuation according to the *Chicago Manual of Style* that I won't understand unless I know what a gerund is, I might have to do a Google search to find out. Because of the intellectual skills I gained through immersing myself in my passion for writing, I can apply myself and figure it out pretty quickly. This would be true even if I hadn't had years of hand cramps after writing twenty sentences and underlining all the nouns once and the verbs twice.

And punctuation! If you're on Facebook, you might have seen this going around.

> Let's eat, Grandma!
> Let's eat Grandma.
> Punctuation saves lives.

It's a funny meme, and those of us who are strong in language arts sometimes pick on people who aren't. Then again, there are a lot of people who would get a good laugh out of watching me trying to change a tire or climb a tree.

Although my two sons were reading at age eleven, their spelling still wasn't the greatest at that point. My husband's spelling still isn't great. The agony of years of public school spelling tests didn't make him a good speller. I attended public school as well, and spelling comes naturally to me. I wouldn't say that school made my husband a horrible speller, nor would I say it made me a good speller. Learning happens everywhere, even in school. Generally, I'd say he's a bad speller in spite of school, and I'm a good speller in spite of school.

When my boys were young teens, we sold things on eBay. I shopped at yard sales and thrift stores then they helped me list and ship the items in the evenings. They each got a percentage of the profits, which was motivation enough to work at writing descriptions that were good enough to sell things. They wrote; I checked and corrected their spelling. As we kept doing that, their writing got better and better until I barely had to correct their writing at all. It was a natural, real world reason to focus on proper spelling and punctuation.

The men in my family still don't have the strong natural language arts talents my daughter and I have, but they do well enough. They know how to look up words they can't spell and how to use spell check. They read articles about things that interest them, have active Twitter accounts, and enjoy manga. Reading and spelling are natural parts of their lives.

My daughter also read much earlier than she mastered spelling. Although she had been reading well from the time she was four years old, it wasn't until she was motivated by a video game at around ten years old that her spelling improved. She enjoyed an online role playing game called *EverQuest*®. Since she didn't go to school, she played during the day when a lot of kids weren't online, so most of the people she played with assumed she was an adult. She led quests and actively participated in her groups, but people sometimes called her names, like Bimbo, because her spelling was good enough for them to assume she was an adult, but an adult who couldn't write well.

She loved that game and took it seriously, so she wanted to be taken seriously as well. She was learning leadership skills and sensing what she needed to do in order to improve herself in an area that was important to her. She began asking me to explain how things were spelled. "What's the difference between two, too, and to? How about there, their, and they're?" She looked up some things herself, asked me lots of questions, and quickly improved. She's now an adult with excellent spelling and writing skills, even though she's never had to take spelling tests and write the words she got wrong ten times. She simply decided one day that she wanted to be a great speller and applied herself. Because of a video game.

Just as some people are more naturally inclined to excel at language, some people are better welders or surfers than others. It's okay to be strong in some areas and weak in others. It's what makes us individuals. The things singled out by schools as The Important Things to Learn are not what are important to every person. In healthy, intellectually stimulating environments, people learn to use the written word at least well enough to do the things that are important to them.

Math

Through the many tear-filled evenings that I struggled to get through math homework as a child, I believed math was too hard, I hated numbers, and I was stupid. I developed a pretty intense math phobia, and that's something I didn't want to pass on to my kids.

I'm certainly not alone in that. It's common to hear an adult laugh and say he can't do math. We don't think anything of it because it's so common. But it's not as socially acceptable to hear an adult say so casually that he can't read. Is that because words are more important than numbers? I don't think so. I think it has more to do with how widespread math phobia is.

There's a lot of talk lately about Common Core math. The way we did math when we were in school is now being called old math. What's funny is that what is now the old math used to be called the new math. And people were really upset about the new math. Parents and grandparents are complaining today that they can't help kids with their Common Core homework because they can't understand the way math is now being taught. I'm not defending Common Core, but I think it's important to remember that schools introduced Common Core because the old math, which used to be the new math, wasn't working. The problem isn't the method they use to pressure kids into learning formal math. The problem is that it's harmful to force a person to learn something that he has no desire or reason to learn.

It comes back to that distinction between intellectual skills and academic skills. School kids don't get much free time to play with numbers and math concepts, and many parents don't set a good example of joyfully playing with math. It's hard to be joyful and playful with numbers after spending our childhoods pressured to master academic skills that had no meaning to us. We were just told to plug numbers into the formulas and get them correct often enough to get a good grade on the tests. We were doing math for the purpose of doing well in school, as opposed to doing it because we saw a value in learning it for our real lives.

My memories of school math are upsetting, but my memories of playing Monopoly® during summer vacation make me smile. I used to set my stuffed animals up around the board and help them take their turns. Things clicked in my head about adding and subtracting that wouldn't click during school. If you give me fifty dollars and tell me to make change for an item that costs eighteen, I've got that in a snap. Not because I filled out math worksheets when I was in school, but because it's like someone bought Kentucky Avenue.

I grew up in a conservative Christian home where tithing all income was a normal part of life. It wasn't a school problem we had to figure out, but something that we just did before we put our money away: 10% goes in one jar, the rest goes in another. Soon I was calculating 10% of my allowance in my head. Once I could figure out 10%, I could figure out almost any other percent. If a sale is 30% off, I figure 10%, then triple it. If I want to know 5%, I still figure 10% in my head and then cut that number in half.

I went shopping once with a friend who has a mental block that percentages are math, and math is hard because she could barely pass math in school. Therefore, she can't figure out percentages unless the store has a chart. The math classes on percentages did nothing but create a negative attitude about them that is still with her as an adult. I tried to explain my method to her, but she looked at me like I was speaking a foreign language. Maybe I couldn't explain it to her because her brain needs to think it through in a completely different way. Maybe I was able to figure it out because I used to sit and play with my money when I was younger. Maybe all my friend would have needed to do to get over her school-induced math block would have been to give herself permission to play with numbers in a way that was meaningful to her. Getting over a mental math block is easier said than done, though. Prevention is the best cure.

My motto with my kids regarding math was, "First, do no harm." I didn't want to pass on my school-induced math anxiety. We played many board games and strategy games through the years, which helped them develop analytical thinking. I could have done more modeling with playing around with numbers than I did, but because I had such severe math phobia I was limited in how much I could do joyfully and playfully. I improved through the years as I learned more about natural learning and the importance of being playful with numbers. I realized that the anxiety, stress, and confusion that I felt about numbers came from a childhood filled with math classes and math testing rather than from an inherent flaw in me. Unschooling my children healed my math phobia to an extent.

In spite of their parents' math issues (my husband graduated from school with similar feelings about math), my adult and teenage children have all the math skills they need to do everything they need and want to do.

My daughter learned addition and subtraction by saving money for an American Girl doll. Give a young child a worksheet with a problem like 100 - (10+1+50) =, and she might not be too happy. But, if a girl has $10 and wants a $100 doll, then her grandpa gives her a dollar, and she gets $50 for her birthday, she has a real reason to be excited about figuring that out.

My daughter now runs a successful business that requires her to make buying decisions based on graphs of past sales patterns, and use software that helps her predict what the ROI (return on investment) of a product would be at different price points.

My sons help list and ship items in my daughter's business. They regularly use math, including listing a product 2% higher than our lowest competitor and weighing and measuring boxes. One time we had several rows of products stacked three high, and my sixteen-year-old was counting 3-6-9-12... I chuckled because this is something little kids are forced to do in school, and he had never been forced to endure those school lessons. Yet there he was doing it.

Maybe he learned it from playing Lego® as a child. Any avid Lego builder knows that three 2 x 2 Lego bricks are the same as one 2 x 6 Lego brick: 3 (2 x 2) = 1 (2 x 6). And although they might not have the academic skill (i.e., know how to plug the numbers into a formula to fill out a worksheet), children who have spent hours and hours building with Lego know intellectually that 1 x 2 + 2 x 2 = 2 x 3, because if you need a 2 x 3 brick and you don't have one, you can substitute a 1 x 2 and a 2 x 2.

Learning math for unschoolers is need-based rather than linear. When a child has a goal, he figures out what he needs and learns it. One of my sons wanted to do some computer programming. He searched on message boards and someone (who obviously had a very schoolish idea of learning that involved a belief that learning must happen through courses taken in a certain order) told him he'd need an algebra class first. So he started taking an algebra course online. He was doing okay with it, but then he started to do actual programming. He realized that what he was told wasn't true. He was programming and not using formal algebra whatsoever. So he quit the algebra class because it wasn't what he needed to take him closer to his goal.

One of the most important things we get from math classes like algebra and trigonometry is analytical reasoning. We can get that analytical reasoning from strategy and brain games. That's probably why someone on a message board told my son that he needed algebra in order to program: for the development of the analytical skills that programming requires. Formal algebra class is not the only way those skills can be developed and, for most people, it's certainly not the best way.

If he or any of my children ever want to learn algebra or trigonometry formally, they can. So far, they haven't chosen to do so. I do know that they do things with X and Y coordinates, which I struggled with in math class, when building things on Minecraft®. Thanks to Battleship®, I understand the basics, but that's about it. My kids tell me there is a Z coordinate, too. They use it and understand it; yet, even though I sat through many math classes and they haven't, I have no clue what they're talking about.

In his book *Free at Last*, Daniel Greenburg tells a story about Sudbury school children who requested that he teach them math classes. Sudbury Valley and other democratic schools like it are sometimes called, "Unschooling schools." Kids in these schools aren't required to take any classes and have as much free time as they need to play outside, play instruments, cook, do art, or whatever they want to do. All decisions regarding school policies and rules are made by students and staff equally. The schools are a true democracy, with staff having no more power over students than students have over staff. Students can request classes from staff members who can choose whether to agree to provide those classes. Greenburg agreed to teach the math class that the kids requested, and they were all able to learn in twenty classroom hours what schools normally take six years to teach. The kids had reasons to want to learn the academic skills, so they did.

There was a time when I wouldn't have believed it if you told me I'd be saying this, but I've come to believe that math isn't that difficult. Forcing kids to do formal academics when they aren't ready, or have no desire, is what makes it difficult. Pressuring them to stay in step with the rest of the class and do well on tests makes it difficult. Math comes naturally as kids play and interact with the real world. Outside those classroom walls are games with probability, sequences, and reasoning. There are thermometers to read, fractions to double in recipes, and symmetry in butterfly wings. There is produce to weigh, money to trade, and percentages to calculate during sales. There are X, Y, and Z coordinates in our Minecraft® maps, music in different time signatures, and geometry in our bowling lanes. Sometimes we find ourselves needing formulas for things that are more involved than we can easily figure out in our heads; and, after much natural use of math, it's not a big deal to apply ourselves to learning to use those formulas.

If you've quizzed your unschooled grandchild (and if you have, please don't do it again—they hate that), and he can't (or won't because he hates to be quizzed) rattle off the answer to 6 x 8, it's okay. He'll be fine.

Unschooling
Doesn't Divide Life Into Subjects

Although I gave an overview of how unschooled kids learn what our society calls "the basics," unschooling families don't divide life into subjects. Anything we do can be a multifaceted learning experience.

We ate at an Italian restaurant once and talked about the map of Italy on our placemats then went home and watched a TV show that serendipitously took place in Milan. Learning happens from everyday things like that all the time. We just make sure that when the kids ask what the map on the placemat is, we tell them. Knowing where Italy is located on a map and viewing some of the landmarks of Italy is what schools would consider geography. But we don't think of our family time as geography class. Unschoolers welcome kids' questions and conversation with them happens often. Not forced, teachy conversation, but interesting, exploratory, sometimes playful conversation. We don't always discuss geography over our placemats. Sometimes we doodle, play tic-tac-toe and hangman, or ignore the placemats altogether. We don't turn everything into a lesson. Learning simply comes as a natural result of living an interesting life. Even visiting family can be valuable.

We live in Pennsylvania, and my brother lives in Boston. When we visit him, we drive through New York and Connecticut. We note with interest, but not with forced schoolishness, that we drive through the capital of Connecticut. In Boston, we strolled along the Charles River, walked the Freedom Trail, ate in Chinatown, and visited the children's museum, where we sat beside Boston Harbor for a lunch break. We stayed at a campground in Massachusetts once, and the GPS told us that it would only take an extra ten minutes of driving to go to the children's museum in Rhode Island before heading home. We didn't need to color in a map on a worksheet to note that Rhode Island borders Massachusetts. If we wanted to assign subjects to the natural learning that occurred in just one trip, we would easily be able to claim geography: Hartford is the capital of Connecticut, Rhode Island borders Massachusetts, and we had firsthand observation of a major river and harbor. Walking the Freedom Trail is history and phys ed. Many subjects are covered in a children's museum. We could count the audio books we listened to in the car as English and the songs we sang in the car as music. There's science in building a campfire and world cultures in visiting Chinatown, but we were just having fun exploring.

Because we don't have a school schedule, we can take day trips as often as we like. Where we live, we can drive to the Liberty Bell or the Statue of Liberty in two or three hours. Sure we can read about historical sites and geographical landmarks in books, but seeing them in person takes it to a whole different level. When you start paying attention, there are all kinds of interesting things to do within a day trip's distance.

Even closer to home, we've explored the woods behind our house and hiked to stripping pits, which are huge pits left behind by surface coal mining. My daughter once found a fossil smack-dab in the middle of our town's soccer field. We live fifteen minutes from Centralia, a town whose residents accidentally set a mammoth vein of coal on fire while burning garbage many years ago, and it's still burning today. We've seen sinkholes and steam coming from the ground. There's science in fossils, history in a mine fire's origins, and geography in exploring stripping pits.

Your family might live near palm trees or rain forests instead of coal mines. Regardless of where your grandkids live or how much they travel, their learning about the world is something they can easily do without formal classes and textbooks.

We do sometimes participate in classes and events held by teachers and experts. We signed up once for a guided night hike through the woods. You can read about animals in a textbook, but that's nothing compared to hiking through the woods in the middle of the night to a porcupine den in hopes of catching a glimpse of the nocturnal animal. We didn't see the porcupine, but we saw his den and evidence that he lived there (poop!).

When my daughter was about ten years old, she asked us to buy her a turtle in a little cup at the fair, so we did. We've had the same turtle in a tank for thirteen years. My son and I went to a workshop about invasive species and found out that our turtle could live to be fifty, which means he'll probably still be around until I'm in my eighties. The turtle has eaten everything we put in with him, including crayfish, toads, snails, and pretty aquarium plants. We went to a state park program about salamanders, and found out that one of the salamanders we sometimes catch (and release) has bright colors that warn predators that it tastes bad. We haven't had the heart to experiment by putting one of those salamanders in the turtle tank to see if he eats it. All this observation of animals and pondering about whether the turtle would eat the red salamander? Science at its best.

We discuss everything, from why spraying a hose into the air makes a rainbow, why the compost pile gets warm, and why Ivory® soap floats. When I don't know the answers, we look them up together.

Fire safety doesn't need to be part of a curriculum if the family regularly changes the batteries in smoke and carbon monoxide detectors, discusses how to be safe as they cook, and talks about what their plan is in a fire or other emergency.

Technology has increased our opportunities to learn interesting things. Facebook didn't even exist until my oldest child was ten years old, and Twitter didn't exist until she was twelve. TV and books introduced us to different world cultures back then, and they still do, but when social media became a big part of our lives, opportunities to learn about other cultures expanded in a big way. The Internet makes conversations with people from different countries possible. When people on Facebook say, "Happy Thanksgiving to my American friends," you realize that American-style Thanksgiving in November doesn't happen everywhere in the world. You begin reading your country's news and politics from the perspective of citizens from other countries, which can be eye-opening. A woman I was close friends with as a teen now lives in Egypt, and I can talk to her as often as I want through Facebook and share stories of her life in Egypt with my family.

We keep up with current events, and when something grabs our attention, we discuss it. When we discussed the debate over South Carolina removing the Confederate flag from their statehouse, history inevitably was a part of the conversation.

It's natural for humans to seek more information when their interest is piqued. If you've ever had a boring teacher drone on and on, or had your eyes glaze over while trying to memorize dates for a history test, you might have an idea why some people's natural inborn sense of curiosity is stifled. The goal of unschooling is to keep it alive and well.

What if All They Want to Do Is Play Video Games?

Some grandparents might say, "Sure, this might work for you because your kids actually get out and learn things. But all my grandkids seem to do is play video games."

They'll be fine. You see, I could spin it two ways. I could tell you that before my son began learning Japanese, he read about how long-term and short-term memory works and came up with a plan based on his research. I could tell you how my teenage boys have been to three symphonies and enjoyed each one. I could mention the programming they've worked with. I could tell you how well they work in the family business.

Or I could tell you that all they want to do is play video games.

Both versions of the story would be true. Because they are such avid video game players, they have pursued interests that came from their passion for video games, but their core passion remains video games.

Because of the hours and hours, day after day, month after month, year after year of video game playing, they naturally became immersed in Japanese things because that's where Nintendo® headquarters is located. That led to their interest in manga and anime, as well as learning Japanese kanji. Studying the language of Japan led them to ask questions about how other languages were developed and the etymology of some of our English words. Because of their love of Japan, I got each of my boys a subscription to Japan Crate for their birthdays, where they get a box of Japanese goodies each month, along with explanations about what the products are and how they're used.

They have Twitter accounts so that they can follow things about video games, and sometimes along the way the video gamers they follow share an interesting article about something else. They listen to podcasts about video games which, as podcasts often do, also talk about off-subject topics.

Their games lead them to Google searches and family conversations about subjects that some people might assume are only ever covered in a classroom. Kid Icarus® is a game based on Greek mythology. Valiant Hearts® is based on World War I. The Professor Layton® series contains mathematical puzzles. Adventure games, such as The Legend of Zelda® series, help with map skills. These aren't "educational" games. They're mainstream video games: the kind that some people say rot kids' brains.

Games don't have to come right out and teach facts in order to be good learning tools. Without prior knowledge of World War I, you might not pick up that the White-Gold Concordat in Skyrim® is analogous to the Treaty of Versailles, but it doesn't take more than a few minutes on an online Skyrim forum to read about that. In Code Name S.T.E.A.M.®, Abraham Lincoln joins forces with the lion from the Land of Oz to defend the queen from an alien invasion. That's not historically accurate, and that's obvious even to a kid who doesn't know much about Abraham Lincoln or English royalty. What it does do is give kids things to wonder about, which often prompts them to look up more about who the historical and fictional characters are. Humans are, by nature, driven by a desire to learn.

The symphonies I mentioned? Video game themed. The music is from the Zelda video games, with footage from the games playing behind the orchestra.

My sons have delved into music many times through the years because of video games. The Zelda series of games has always been, and remains, a favorite. The main character in the game, Link, plays an ocarina, so they bought ocarinas and taught themselves to play them. We learned about many musical instruments by listening to people playing some of their favorite video game music on YouTube®, first on ocarinas, and then on guitar, piano, violin, harp, marimba, you name it.

They took guitar lessons for a while, and Luke took piano and trumpet lessons as well. Their sole reason for learning new instruments was to learn to play Zelda songs.

We went to the Renaissance Faire because the Zelda games have a very medieval feel to them. While there, Luke bought a pan flute and learned to play it.

The reason Luke took horseback riding lessons was so he could ride a horse like Link. We found the most awesome teacher in the world who was even willing to put the cones he was supposed to ride around in the shape of a triforce, a symbol from the game.

I helped him sew a costume, which involved math, so that he could look like Link while he rode. Then we made foam shields and wooden shields with a jig saw. We made rupee bags (rupees are the currency in the Zelda games). We hiked through the woods with our shields, going on adventures just like Link.

We used Sculpey® clay to make triforces and our own ocarinas. We painted on magnifying glasses to make the Lens of Truth. We made cake pops that looked like Koopa shells and cooked up some pumpkin soup, a delicacy in one of the Zelda games.

I took them to PAX East in Boston, which is a huge video game conference. While there, they were able to play many indie games before they went on the market, attend a panel of video game developers who talked about their careers, and hear one of their favorite podcasts live. While we were there, they had their first Pho from a Vietnamese restaurant and fish and chips from a British restaurant.

Some of the first words they read were video game-related, and some of their earliest reading was video game guides.

They've always enjoyed making up their own levels in games, from the time they were little and played Freddi Fish. They spent days making elaborate Lego versions of Mario Party games, complete with their own minigames. This inspired them to work on an idea for a video game they might like to develop themselves, which led them to learn programming.

Sure they work hard selling things in our family business—so they can buy video games. Even when they were younger, they gave a lot of thought (thought that involved arithmetic) to which video games they would spend their birthday and Christmas money on.

I never sat down and said, "Today, we're going to learn about instruments!" or "Our next project will be sewing a costume!" I didn't even say, "Why don't you pick a video game-related art project to do?"

I never said we had to supplement their video game playing with academic things or told them that they had to "learn something" today. I trusted that they were learning all the time and that their interests would take them wherever they needed to go. When someone said, "I wish I could ride a horse like Link," I considered how we might be able to make that happen. If they were interested in my ideas, we did them.

If your grandkids seem to be playing a lot of video games, don't worry. They're learning.

Chapter Four

Socialization

Socialization is sometimes a concern of grandparents. Either they think the kids don't get out enough and are socially awkward, or they think the kids spend too much time playing with friends and not enough time doing schoolwork.

You'll come to a place of peace with your family's unschooling much easier and quicker if you accept that socialization, as well as every other area of concern, will look different in unschooled kids. The kids will be different, the way the family does things will be different. They aren't square pegs trying to squeeze into round holes. They are square pegs celebrating the fact that they are square and not making any attempt or showing any desire whatsoever to have anything to do with holes they don't fit into. Unschooling follows a child's lead in matters of socialization as well as academics. Different people need different things.

The world of school values extroverts, as long as they don't talk to their classmates during class or while they're in line or spend too much time playing with friends after school instead of quietly doing homework. It values those who are so eager to participate in a group that they readily accept commands of when to sit and when to stand, who eagerly raise their hands and answer questions, who are outgoing and popular with teachers and fellow students, and who stay after school for sports, band, or other after-school activities. There's a "successful" mold that kids are supposed to try to fit into, and the better a kid fits into the mold, the more successfully socialized he is considered to be.

But unschooling values uniqueness. If you're concerned about a kid who doesn't want to go out much, or one who wants to be constantly on the go, know that some kids are introverts and some are extroverts, and that's okay. It's actually more than okay. The human race has introverts and extroverts for a reason: They both offer the world different and important things. When a child has one good friend who he gets together with once every few weeks and prefers to spend the rest of his time at home alone, that's perfectly okay. If the child wants his schedule filled with outside activities and a constant flow of people, even to the point that it seems like he's never home, that's perfectly okay, too. It's an unschooling parent's job to make sure that each child's unique social needs are respected and met, just as much as it is to make sure he or she provides the unique learning resources and opportunities that each child requires.

In school, kids are forced to associate with whoever is in their classes, which is usually based on their age, where their last name falls alphabetically, what town they live in, or how well they do on tests. Unschooled kids can choose their friends in much the same way adults can: based on personality and interests, from a wider pool of people than just those they're forced into a classroom with. Sure they can play with kids who live in the same community if they find they enjoy their company. They can also play with kids in homeschool and unschooling groups. There are community groups where people with common interests can get together regardless of age. The Internet allows us to interact with people from all over the world.

Another thing that happens sometimes with concerned grandparents is that they don't realize how often their grandkids get together with other kids. I've seen families withdraw from sharing things with grandparents to avoid criticism, or what they perceive as criticism, by not sharing much of their day-to-day life with the grandparents. They just don't want to feel judged. So it could be that your grandkids' socialization looks a lot different than you think it does. They could be going to playground dates, unschooling gatherings, taking day trips to interesting places, and meeting friends for lunch.

One thing I've done with my kids, and now my daughter does it with her kids as well, is visit many different libraries. As a matter of fact, I have a stack of library cards so big I have to have a separate little coin purse to hold all of them. My daughter and I once took her kids to a library about an hour from our house because they'd advertised a special event that looked interesting. One of my grandkids enjoyed the program and the other didn't, so my daughter stayed with the one who wanted to do the program, and I explored the library with the other one. Unschooling parents' goal of making sure each child gets what he needs can be made easier by involved grandparents. We were delighted to discover that the library has a very nice children's section with toys, board games, and activities. While we were there, we ran into another family we know from a homeschool group. The kids played Connect 4® and talked about their favorite movies. They played for quite a long time. If I hadn't been an involved grandma, I might have only known that the grandkids stopped at a library, if I even knew that. Ho-hum. Poor unsocialized, unschooled kids whose highlight of their week is getting library books.

When unschoolers get together, they can spend as much or as little time as their individual needs require. Unschoolers can stay all day at playgrounds or other get-togethers because they don't have to get up for school in the morning. Playdates don't have to be limited to recess or weekends after homework and extracurricular activities.

In the book *Quiet: The Power of Introverts in a World That Can't Stop Talking* by Susan Cain (which I highly recommend to anyone wanting to understand more about introverts and how they work), she talks about the "Extrovert Ideal," which she describes as "the omnipresent belief that the ideal self is gregarious, alpha, and comfortable in the spotlight." She says, "We like to think that we value individuality, but all too often we admire one type of individual—the kind who's comfortable 'putting himself out there.'" And she says, "Introversion—along with its cousins, sensitivity and shyness—is now a second-class personality trait, somewhere between a disappointment and a pathology. Introverts living under the Extrovert Ideal are like women in a man's world, discounted because of a trait that goes to the core of who they are."

Unschooling is all about celebrating who a person is and encouraging people to be fully themselves. In unschooling, there is no "Extrovert Ideal." There is a "Whoever you are at your core is ideal." That is the most emotionally healthy ideal because it's what best allows both introverts and extroverts to contribute who they really are to the world.

How do we know if our kids need to spend more time alone or more time in social situations? We trust them. We give them the space and freedom to listen to their own inner voices and we let them act on them. We don't tell them what we've planned for them and what we expect of them. Rather, we observe who they are and offer things based on what we think might be a good fit for them. We tell them about events and activities they might enjoy. We accept it when they say no. When they tell us they'd love to go to a concert instead, we take them.

My daughter's kids get bored if they stay home too much, but my teens like to stay home because they get bored when they leave the house. I celebrate each of them for who they are and encourage them to spend their time doing what is true to them.

Meeting each child's unique needs isn't always an easy job, especially when a parent is trying to meet individual needs of different children. Sometimes a mom has the challenge of how to get Child One to her art club at 2:00, which is the same time Child Two has to be picked up from her activity at the state park, which is half an hour away. And sometimes, amidst all the hustle to get to everyone's activities, she has to go grocery shopping for snacks because Child Three has a friend coming over later that day. Anyone who asks that mom about socialization will get an eye roll at best, and a good telling-off at worst. Perhaps unschooling parents should be more patient in explaining their lifestyle to those who aren't familiar with unschooling, and should perhaps ask for help when they need it, but might feel they don't have the time or the energy to deal with potential criticism. If that's the kind of activity level your family has, the mom will probably weep grateful tears if you ask how you can help her juggle all that.

When my daughter was a teen, she spent a lot of time alone playing video games, which would concern some grandparents. Except that she wasn't really alone. She was very involved in an online role-playing game where she regularly got together with people to do things. (I never got very involved with her game, so "do things" is about as descriptive as I can get. I didn't need to understand everything about her game to respect that it was something she enjoyed and therefore had value.) She took a leadership role in that game, organizing online groups of people to go on virtual adventures.

I learned that even if I enticed her to join us for some really cool activity, if she had an appointment to meet with other people to "do stuff" in her game, it was a real commitment that was important to her and that she took seriously. If she had a game commitment at 6:00, I made sure to get her home in time. Not just because I wanted to encourage her to be the kind of person who shows up when she says she will, but because I wanted to be respectful of her.

My grandkids want to go somewhere constantly. They love to explore new places, and they enjoy free play with other kids. We fill our schedules with playgrounds, lakes, swimming pools, children's museums, science museums, and play dates. We don't just take them out once or twice a week. They are extroverts who need to be out a lot as much as introverts need to be home a lot. People sometimes ask my daughter why they're always going somewhere. The answer is simple: That's how they shine.

Don't try to change your grandchild or measure him against an ideal of what you think a kid should be. It's so much nicer to ease into having a relationship with the children and grandchildren we have than the children and grandchildren we wish we had or think we should have. We don't really need to understand all the biological or psychological aspects of why an introvert wants to stay home, or an extrovert feels the need to hang out with a friend after having just spent the last twelve hours at a sleepover. We might not understand why an introvert suddenly wants to get out of the house more often. We might not understand why our grandkids suddenly don't want to spend as much time with a particular child or group of friends. But we can trust the children to follow their intuition and know exactly what they need. If they are trusted to follow their intuition and supported by adults committed to meeting their needs, they will thrive.

Chapter Five

Testing, Quizzing, and Grading

Unschooled kids learn from everyday situations. They learn to challenge themselves, in their own time and in their own way, and we give them the space to do so. They don't need us to challenge them in the way that schools do, with quizzes, tests, and grades. We don't criticize or tell them they don't know something well enough. You might have noticed that your unschooling family gets particularly defensive if you quiz the kids on what they know. They see it as a challenge to their chosen lifestyle and their parenting, but there's also a deeper reason. Quizzing conflicts strongly with the philosophy of unschooling.

Unschoolers don't want their kids to lose the drive to experiment and question that they had when they were two and three years old. An F can certainly discourage a child and hurt his self-esteem, but working for an A can cause its own set of problems. Alfie Kohn says in his bio on his blog that he writes and speaks about research in human behavior, education, and parenting. On his DVD, *No Grades + No Homework = Better Learning*, he says, "What studies find over and over again is the more you reward students for doing something, the more they tend to lose interest in whatever they had to do to get the reward. No wonder the research finds, consistently, that students trying to get A's tend to be less interested in learning as a result of that fact."

A child who works hard for A's spends his time doing what someone else wants him to do, to meet external demands to get an external reward. The need for an A takes the focus off of what he's learning and onto what he needs to do to get the desired grade. It doesn't give him much time to get to know himself, to do things to satisfy his own innate drive to learn and explore the things that call to him.

John Holt, in his book *How Children Fail*, talks about what can happen when a child is often challenged and quizzed. "The anxiety children feel at constantly being tested, their fear of failure, punishment, and disgrace, severely reduces their ability both to perceive and to remember, and drives them away from the material being studied into strategies for fooling teachers into thinking they know what they really don't know."

I did just that in school. I had a lot of anxiety about grades because I had bought into the idea that if I got good grades, I was somehow more worthy. People thought I was a good kid because I got good grades, but I knew a secret that made me (or so I thought) both stupid and a fraud: I had to study harder for good grades than some other people. I didn't want others to see how stupid I felt, or to catch on that I really wasn't as worthy to be considered a good kid. So, in addition to studying hard to get good grades (I really didn't care much at all about the actual content, as long as I could memorize it and regurgitate it for a test), I was smart enough to figure out which classes were easiest while still giving the highest number of points so that I could rank well percentage-wise when I graduated. I learned to smile sweetly, raise my hand, and act interested whether or not I liked the teacher or cared about the topic being discussed.

A system that labels kids as "good" or "bad" based on their willingness to jump through the right hoops to get the right grades, or on how cunning their ability is to manipulate the system, and places a high importance on that label, encourages a degree of dishonesty and a lack of personal integrity.

Unschoolers care about their children's characters. They tend to not care as much about putting on appearances, but focus on authenticity. They care about a child being honest with himself and focusing his thoughts, creativity, and research on what truly appeals to him mentally and emotionally.

Unschooled kids find pleasure in learning. When they put extra effort into learning something that is important to them, the push comes from inside themselves, from their own internal desire. If an unschooling parent seems defensive if you quiz her child, know that she is coming from a place of wanting to protect her child. Quizzing goes against everything she believes will best help her child learn and grow.

Chapter Six

Deschooling

There is a concept called deschooling that might apply if your grandkids were recently taken out of school. Deschooling is the process that occurs when someone unlearns the way school has shaped their thinking in regard to learning. If your unschooled grandkids recently left school and it seems like all they want to do is sit around and do nothing, they might just need time to deschool. When a student is burned out from all the forced studying and cramming of information they didn't care about so they could pass tests, it takes time to decompress from that. Kids are born with a flame of learning burning bright, but their flame of learning might be down to a barely recognizable spark. They might see learning as something they have to do, as a chore they have to force themselves to endure in order to avoid the negative consequences of bad grades and schoolish judgment. They might barely be able to muster up the curiosity to care enough if something they read or hear really is true. If a person is really entrenched in the system, researching, pondering, and exploring might only matter to her if her actions will propel her forward toward a good grade, an honor roll, a degree, or a title.

Deschooling will allow such a child the time to transition into the rhythm of unschooling. Once she has deschooled, her mindset will have changed. Her goal in pursuing learning will be for the joy of learning itself or for the purpose of moving her farther toward a goal that she has set for herself. Chances are, her goal probably has little to do with being recognized by the system. Unschoolers often say to expect one to three months for every year of formal schooling before learning really starts to look the way it does in unschoolers. It's not that he won't be learning anything during that time, it's just that the learning won't look the same as it would in someone who has always been unschooled.

Chapter Seven

Radical Unschooling

Whereas unschooling is about completely trusting the natural learning process, radical unschooling, or whole life unschooling, takes trusting children further. They are trusted to listen to their bodies about things like what they eat, when they go to bed, and what they wear. They make their own decisions about how to spend their days and with whom. Not without any guidance or mentoring, of course. Unschooled kids spend a great deal of time one-on-one with parents and other adults. They talk about principles: kindness, compassion, patience, responsibility, etc. But there are no arbitrary rules.

As I explained in Chapter One, not all unschoolers are radical unschoolers, although for many, the longer they unschool, the more they progress to the radical end of the spectrum.

As I cover each aspect of radical unschooling, also keep in mind that there are people who parent the same way in some of these areas who aren't unschoolers at all. For example, I know parents of schooled kids who use the same approach to food freedom or don't punish their children.

Some unschoolers embrace some aspects of radical unschooling but not others. Chances are, if your family are unschoolers, a lot of this is going to look familiar. Take what applies and leave the rest.

Behavior

Just as we don't punish or reward for grades, radical unschoolers don't punish or reward for behavior.

Some people use reward charts to get their kids to clean up, use good manners, or brush their hair. Radical unschoolers don't, for the same reason they don't give grades and gold stars for academic performance. It's a carrot-and-stick approach, using manipulation to change external behavior rather than focusing on internal thoughts and motives. Rewards for behavior can sometimes temporarily change external behavior, but don't mentor a child so that he develops his internal moral code on which he bases his behavior.

Even praise, when used as a reward to motivate future good behavior, can be dangerous. Catch him doing a good deed and praise him for it, and you run the risk of teaching him to only do good deeds when he's likely to get praise. You weaken his internal motivation and strengthen his desire for external motivation. You send him the message that he can't be trusted to be good enough on his own, so he needs to be controlled. Depending on his personality, he might resent that message and rebel. Or, worse yet, he might internalize the belief that he can't listen to himself and needs to base his actions on what will please others.

There's a difference between saying positive things in the spirit of support and celebration with someone who accomplished something important to them and saying positive things because you think your statements will get them to do more of what you think they should do. If a child worked hard on a self-portrait and proudly shows it to you, and you're genuinely impressed, tell her so. But pointing out how a child colored a part of his coloring page inside the lines in hopes that he'll color in the lines more often is manipulation.

We talk about how characters on TV and in books feel about how someone treated them, and that helps us be mindful of how we treat people. We talk about how we would feel if someone hurt us or destroyed something that was important to us, and that helps us not do it to others. We don't lecture our kids about these things, but they come up naturally in conversation. We are their adult partners, not the adults who police them. We've lived in this world longer than they have, so we can often give good advice, but our authority is a natural authority, not a forced authority. Children naturally look to their parents and other adults for support and guidance when they're not looking at them as people to avoid so they don't get punished. In order to help our children develop good character and a strong internal code of behavior, we don't have to spank, use time-outs, ground them, or take away personal possessions.

The end goal isn't about simply changing behavior in the moment. The end goal is a person who has developed her character and knows and respects herself so well that when she acts, she is acting out of her own firmly developed internal convictions.

Sometimes grandparents see unschooled kids behaving in a way that they would have punished, and they don't understand the way an unschooling parent reacts.

First, unschooling parents aren't perfect. If they weren't raised without punishment and rewards, this is new to them, too. It could be that the parent just messed up, or isn't sure how to handle a situation.

However, while I've never known an unschooling parent who claimed to be perfect, they do spend a lot of time thinking about how to deal with different child behaviors in respectful ways. Chances are, if you're disapproving of the way they react to a child's behavior, it's because they are operating from a different philosophy.

In some situations, they might see the behavior differently than you and not categorize it as bad. If a kid jumps in a puddle and gets his shoes wet: Bad behavior or not?

My answer from a radical unschooling perspective is that it's not bad behavior. The act of jumping in water is neutral morally and ethically. Getting shoes wet is also morally and ethically neutral, even though it can leave you cold and uncomfortable if you have to walk around in wet sneakers.

What if a child was told by an adult not to jump into the puddle?

I would still say it's not bad behavior, and I would also say that the goal of an unschooling parent or grandparent isn't obedience. We might say, "Watch out for the puddle" to someone who we know doesn't want to get wet. And while we try to have the wisdom and foresight to bring extra clothes and shoes because of the propensity of small children to do things like jump in puddles, we might find ourselves in a situation where we don't have spares with us. In such a case, we would just remind them that we don't have spares with us and that if they jump in the puddle, they'll get wet. If they jump anyway, then a natural consequence is being wet until we're able to get them dry shoes. If they complain, we won't say, "I told you so," because no one likes someone who says that. We can still be loving and sympathetic in such a situation because we've all done things against our better judgment. Have we not all as adults, at one time or another, eaten the food that we know is going to make our bellies uncomfortable or stayed up too late reading a good book, even though we knew we would regret it when the alarm rang?

Now, if a child splashes someone who doesn't want to be splashed, either out of meanness or simply disregarding the desires and comforts of another person, that's no longer morally and ethically neutral. He can't push his sister into the puddle, no matter how mad she makes him. We stop the behavior, we remove him from the situation if necessary, and we talk to him about why. Such intervention is needed much more often in the toddler years than it is for older children because, through the years, we have helped them mindfully consider their actions and the feelings of others.

While we might occasionally have to remove a child from a situation to keep him from hurting himself or others, we never have to punish him or shame him. No standing in the corner, no spanking, no threats of being put on Santa's naughty list. We don't want them to behave a certain way just to avoid punishment. Our goals run deeper than that.

Manipulating kids' behavior trains them to manipulate a system to avoid punishment or gain more reward. It teaches them to obey whoever happens to be in authority over them, but it doesn't teach them to stand up for themselves and their own values. What happens if a child has been taught to always obey adults then an adult asks him to do something sexual? When a boss asks him to do something unethical or illegal?

Unschooled kids uphold themselves to their own standards and convictions. One time my kids and I were at a McDonald's play place. There were many kids there that day, and some of them got into a fight. My kids weren't involved. The mother of a kid who got hurt put her hands on her hips and yelled that she wanted every single kid out of the play place right now, and she wanted them all lined up so she could figure out exactly who had hit her kid. My kids, I'm proud to say, ignored her and kept playing. They knew that they didn't have to obey her, especially when she was yelling so disrespectfully. My kids respect others, but they also expect to be respected. When she saw that they weren't complying with her demands, and that I wasn't enforcing her demands like the other parents were, she knew she didn't have a leg to stand on and had to settle for screaming at the kids who had come to stand before her.

My daughter and I took her kids to a weeklong pirate day camp at a local children's museum. Overall, they really enjoyed it, but there was a point one day when a lot of the kids were getting antsy. Demonstrations had gone on a little too long, and the story wasn't interesting them. Other parents and grandparents sternly told their kids that they must sit and listen to the teacher. One even said, "You need to learn how to listen, you're going to school next year." When my grandson started getting antsy, he and I left the pirate camp to play elsewhere in the museum. His mom stayed and texted me when they moved on to an activity she thought he'd enjoy. His leaving during the boring part didn't disrupt the program or bother anyone, except maybe the moms and grandmas who were working so hard to prepare their kids for school by making them sit and listen to something they didn't want to be doing.

I've attended workshops where I left because the workshop wasn't as helpful to me as I had thought it would be, I wasn't feeling well, or something more urgent needed my attention. Kids deserve to be able to make the same kinds of decisions they'll be able to make when they're adults. We don't want to train them to accept what they don't want. We want them to grow up to be people who passionately love their work and spend their days doing what they love, and only sit through the boring stuff if they've decided that the boring stuff helps them meet their goals.

Some people have one set of rules for adults and another for kids. They expect kids to say "Yes, sir" or "Yes, ma'am," while adults address them any way they want. Some adults don't think twice about interrupting kids, but would never let kids interrupt adults. They believe that children should be seen and not heard. Children aren't a lower class, they're not a bother, and they're not a mere distraction from the important things that grown-ups do. They're equally valuable human beings with very important ideas. We should take them seriously.

That's why our family works to arrange our schedules so the kids' needs are honored as much as the adults'. I knew they would want to stay longer at the museum after pirate camp, so I brought my laptop so I could sit in a corner writing while they played. I took the occasional break to help the kids by putting a Lego® guy into a car and buttoning a dress-up costume, but I wrote half a chapter while I was there. What I want and need to do is important, but so is what they want and need to do. Imagine if all children grew up knowing how to work together so that everyone was respected and their needs were met.

Before we tell our kids they shouldn't do something, we think very carefully why we might say that. Is it actually wrong? If we know why they're doing what they're doing, can they get the desired outcome if they tweak their actions? Are we telling them no because it's easier for us that way, or because we're worried about what others might think?

We try to say yes more than we say no. I often ask myself, "Why not?" or "How can I let them do what they're really wanting to do?" Does a child want to stay up to watch one more show, read one more chapter, or play with Lego® for one more hour? Why not? Being a night owl isn't morally or ethically wrong. If he wants to climb up the slide, why not? As long as no one is on the way down.

That doesn't mean we don't obey the rules of the public or private places we go. If we know our kids aren't able to sit still for long periods of time at sit-down restaurants, we don't go to them. We might order takeout and eat at a park instead. If we do end up at a restaurant and a child is having a hard time being still and quiet, we might help them by letting them watch YouTube® on our phones, taking them outside to walk around the block, or even taking them home. Not as a punishment, but as a way to help them find a place where they're able to act appropriately. We don't need to yell or punish in order to keep our kids from running around a restaurant. When they're older and understand why and how to act in a restaurant, they will. No need to subject them to something they're not ready for when they're little.

If a sign says don't walk on the grass, we don't walk on it, even if it seems like a stupid and petty rule.

If the museum says not to touch the display, we don't touch it, no matter how much we want to. Our town has a noise ordinance, so we can't play loud music outside after midnight.

When we go to other people's houses, we respect their rules when they differ from ours. At our house, kids can jump on the furniture and carry their red Kool-Aid® into the living room, but not everyone allows that. Some people want shoes taken off at the front door. Some people expect kids to clean up all the toys before they leave and others would prefer to do it themselves so they're sure things get put back in the correct places. We respect others' homes and their individual ways of doing things on their own private property. We talk about what we expect the rules to be like before we get to someone's house so there are fewer surprises. If a child finds the rules somewhere else to be too restrictive, we avoid going there.

The only things we insist on in our family are that you don't hurt people or infringe on their property and you don't do illegal things. You can run around naked at home, but it's not allowed in public. Whether or not it's morally wrong to do so doesn't matter if the law forbids nudity. You can, however, wear pajamas or your favorite costume to the store. If you're little enough, you can probably get away without shoes if an adult carries you or you sit in the cart. And people in barefoot societies usually know the laws regarding being barefoot in public. Sometimes we're legally allowed to do more than we realize.

In other words, completely think through everything that you do or don't do. Don't be rude or disrespectful, but don't let other people be rude or disrespectful to you just because you're little either. Yes, even if you're a child, you can expect an adult to say, "Excuse me," if he must interrupt your conversation or walk between you and your friend.

Unless there's a law or rule saying that you can't, and as long as there isn't a legitimate safety reason not to, it's okay to take off your shoes and wade in the creek, even if other parents tell their kids they can't. You don't have to obey other kids' parents unless it's a rule about their personal property.

It's okay to use marker to draw on your skin instead of your paper. There are no ethical, moral, or legal reasons not to. It will wash off eventually. No, you can't draw on another kid's skin or paper, at least not without his permission. But your own skin belongs to you. Want to get your nose pierced? Same principle—it's your body. I'd help my kids research so they know how to take care of the piercing properly, and I'd make sure the piercing parlor uses the cleanest, safest practices.

Parents and grandparents of kids who are free sometimes get strange looks (and even glares!) from other parents. So be it. We don't believe in following the crowd just for the sake of keeping up appearances. We're more principled than that. I've also witnessed other parents relaxing about what they let their kids do when they see that we don't expect the restrictions, as though they were only restricting their kids for the sake of being accepted.

While we don't punish, there are natural consequences. If you stay up late and you choose to get up in the morning to go somewhere, you might be tired. Next time, maybe you'll go to bed earlier. Or maybe not. We don't punish a child for not going to bed, or create a "natural consequence" by arbitrarily making them get up at a certain time. The choice to get up early or not is theirs. Natural consequences aren't created by the parents to teach a lesson, or they're not natural. Natural consequences happen by themselves.

The natural consequence of eating while dinner is being prepared might be that you're not hungry when the rest of the family is hungry. That's not a horrible consequence because you can always ask for food to be saved for you to warm up later, but it is a consequence. A natural consequence is not, "You missed dinner with the family, so now you have to go to bed hungry." That's a punishment rather than a natural consequence.

The natural consequence to being yourself could be that some people don't approve of your child or your family. It might mean that you don't get invited to playdates with that group of people. And that's what usually happens when you are true to yourself. You end up surrounded by people who are drawn to your true, authentic self, and those who don't resonate with who you are tend to go away.

The natural consequence of adults respecting children is children who understand the importance of respect because they know what respect feels like.

One big issue with their kids' grandparents that I hear unschoolers talk about is that the grandparents don't respect the unschooling way of disciplining. They pick their kids up from Grandma's house to hear that the child was put in time-out, threatened that they won't get a cookie if they don't finish their lunch, or bribed with a special toy for trying to read something or perform some academic task. That will put a rift in your relationship with an unschooled family. If this is radically different than what you're used to, rest assured that you're not the only one who needs some time to get used to it.

It took a few years for me to fully incorporate all aspects of radical unschooling with my kids. In the area of discipline, what it took was a firm decision on my part that I would simply not, no matter what happens, yell at my kids.

My kids tell me my weak spot is a special tone in my voice where I kind of "talk down" to people I'm frustrated with. I do this with adults, too. "Sure, you don't yell," my daughter said. "But you use this tone that tells me you think I'm an idiot." I have to watch that. Going cold turkey from yelling at my kids worked well for me, but I still had to learn to think mindfully about every situation and to remain respectful in my thoughts about the other person, or the agitation in my head would come out as a condescending tone instead of yelling. A condescending tone can be just as bad, maybe sometimes even worse, than yelling.

If you've spent your whole life—as many of us have—believing that kids need to be yelled at, threatened, punished, rewarded, or in some way coerced to make their behavior acceptable, it's very hard to change your paradigm. It can be done, though, by mindfully considering the respect that children deserve as human beings.

While an unschooling family will probably get upset if you offer a bribe to get your grandchild to learn something or behave differently, that doesn't mean you can't have a positive influence on his character development. He'll learn about kindness by watching you be kind to the waitress. He'll learn about patience when you're patient with him. He'll learn about perseverance when he sees you not giving up and maintaining a good attitude when you're learning a new game. He'll learn about honesty when he sees you find a wallet and return it to its owner. Your own example is powerful.

Food Freedom

Radical unschoolers let their kids choose what food they put into their bodies.

When I was transitioning to radical unschooling, food was one of the last areas of control I surrendered. I was big on making sure my kids got enough fruits and veggies, and I monitored their intake pretty closely.

"It hurts my throat," my son said one day when I tried to get him to eat cantaloupe.

I told him he was being silly, making up excuses. "It's good for you! Eat it!"

And then I saw the hives around his lips. He was allergic to cantaloupe, and I hadn't known it. But he knew instinctively: Don't eat this. It doesn't make my body feel good.

That was the last time I ever controlled what my kids ate. I had been reading about radical unschooling and food freedom for a while, so the background understanding was laid, and I was able to instantly transition. While most kids aren't going to have an allergic reaction to something their parents are trying to force them to eat, it's important that kids learn to pay attention to which foods work best with their unique bodies. It's the same reason that grades can hurt learning. Make kids work for an A, all they'll care about is getting the A. Make kids eat their veggies before they get the cupcake, all they'll care about is the cupcake. The allure of the cupcake becomes enhanced, and the veggies become even more distasteful, an obstacle to overcome to get to the reward.

Praise for a clean plate doesn't fit well with the radical unschooling philosophy, nor does guilt. Kids in Africa can't be fed what a kid in America leaves behind on his plate.

I have some issues with compulsive eating and eating as stress relief. Just like I had because of my math phobia, I developed a "First, do no harm" policy with food. There was a lot of room for improvement in my own diet, yet I was trying to micromanage theirs. Not too smart.

Research about kids and healthy eating supports the radical unschooling approach to food freedom. In a

March 27, 2015, article entitled "Keep Kids Out of the Clean Plate Club," Ximena Jimenez, MS, RDN, a spokesperson for the Academy of Nutrition and Dietetics, talks about the importance of not forcing kids to overeat so they don't lose the ability to read their internal hunger cues.

www.eatright.org/resource/food/nutrition/eating-as-a-family/keep-kids-out-of-the-clean-plate-club

The *WebMD* article "Why praising Kids With Food Doesn't Work" explains why using food, especially desserts, as a reward can be harmful. "You encourage a desire for sweets and poor eating habits. Giving children food for good behavior teaches them to eat whether or not they are actually hungry, the Connecticut State Department of Education reports. You send the message that sweets are more valuable than other foods."

www.webmd.com/parenting/features/why-praising-kids-with-food-doesnt-work

Food freedom has worked well in my family, and it's worked well in the families of other radical unschoolers I've talked with. We provide a variety of foods, and we trust them to follow their hunger cues and eat when they're hungry rather than eating when the clock reads a certain time. Kids who grow up with food freedom learn to self-regulate. Sure, they might sometimes choose to eat cake for dinner, or have occasional binges on candy and soda. But overall, they learn what feels right and what doesn't, and learn to eat a diet that is balanced and healthy for their own bodies.

In order for kids to learn self-control, they need to be able to control themselves. Otherwise, they're simply complying with someone else's control over them.

Sleep Freedom

Just as we trust kids to listen to their bodies in regard to what foods they eat, we trust them to listen to their bodies in regard to their sleep. It's not uncommon for parents of school kids, especially teenagers, to have a hard time getting them out of bed in the morning. Beyond the fact that some kids might be unmotivated to get up because they dread going to school, scientists have known for years that there is a biological reason.

A January 10, 2006, *Washington Post* article entitled "Schools Waking Up to Teens' Unique Sleep Needs" reports a sleep study done by Brown University Professor Mary Carskadon. She encourages schools to change their start times to be more in line with teenagers' natural body rhythms, because teens are biologically driven to have later sleep times.

www.washingtonpost.com/wp-dyn/content/article/2006/01/09/AR2006010901561.html

"Carskadon, who teaches human behavior and is director of sleep research at E.P. Bradley Hospital in Rhode Island, led a team of researchers who helped prove that—biologically speaking—teenagers really are out of it early in the morning.

The researchers measured the presence of the sleep-promoting hormone melatonin in teenagers' saliva at different times of the day. They learned that the melatonin levels rise later at night than they do in children and adults—and remain at a higher level later in the morning."

Sleep research on teens continues to show similar results. A November 7, 2014, article on the Brown University website, entitled "Sleep Starts Later as Teens Age, But School Still Starts Early," tells of another study done by Carskadon and her fellow researchers. "This is one of the few studies that has tracked sleep behavior and circadian rhythms over the course of up to two-and-a-half years in the same adolescents," said lead author Stephanie Crowley. "The study showed that while sleep cycles of kids get later and later as they age, they still are forced to get up early for school. Of course, that leads to a sleep deficit that isn't good for them."

Unfortunately, with few exceptions, schools haven't listened to this advice. Even if they had, though, and schools started later in the day, they wouldn't be taking into account the fact that each body is different. Some people need more sleep than others. Some people are morning people and some people aren't, and it's important that we honor each person's unique sleep needs.

A March 18, 2016, vox.com article entitled "If You're Just Not a Morning Person, Science Says You May Never Be" explains the scientific reasons for respecting the sleep patterns of both night owls and early birds: We all have a unique chronotype, which is when our bodies want to fall asleep. "It turns out our internal clocks are influenced by genes and are incredibly difficult to change. If you're just not a morning person, it's likely you'll never be, at least until the effects of aging kick in. And what's more, if we try to live out of sync with these clocks, our health likely suffers. The mismatch between internal and real world time has been linked to heart disease, obesity, and depression."

www.vox.com/2016/3/18/11255942/morning-people-evening-chronotypes-sleeping

Research backs up what radical unschoolers do instinctively: simply trust a child to listen to his own body.

Chores

Most radical unschooling parents try to set an example of joy in all things they do. We don't do anything because we have to, but because we want to. We do the laundry because we love our family and want them to have clean clothing to wear. We do the dishes because we love our family and are glad that we were able to feed them. Mindfulness is huge in radical unschooling. We strive to think through why we do every single thing that we do.

When our kids help us, we want them to do so willingly and joyfully. We don't force them to help, but we sometimes ask our kids for help the same way we would ask our spouses for help. The older they are, and the more respectfully they've been treated, the more likely that they will be willing to help.

I once had a conversation with someone who didn't understand why I don't just make kids do as they're told.

"What if," she asked, "you had a six-year-old who made a huge mess, threw toys all over the place, had crumbs all over the floor, and you asked him to clean it up and he wouldn't? Wouldn't you tell him he couldn't watch TV until it was cleaned up?"

I told her that I don't punish my kids, and that I don't force chores.

She looked at me like I had three heads, so I went on to give her an example. The night before our conversation, we were getting ready for carpet cleaners. There was still quite a bit of work to do, including decluttering, moving furniture, and vacuuming. I said that I was getting tired, and that I might just go to bed and finish early the next morning. My sixteen-year-old son, without anyone asking him to, said that he would also get up to help.

"But," she said, "We're not talking about a teen, we're talking about a six-year-old. How would you make the six-year-old clean up?"

I wouldn't.

Instead of telling him to clean it up, I would clean it up for him, and I would welcome him to join me. I would try to remember to be cheerful about getting the house in order. Housework is anything but my strong point, and I have some very negative attitudes about housework that I don't want to pass on to my kids, so I consciously work on my attitude. I might "let" the child use the vacuum hose to suck stuff up, since six-year-old kids tend to enjoy that. I might talk about the toys as I work. "I remember when your grandma got you this." Or I might say, "Let's get these cleaned up before we bake those cookies. Can you put your cars away while I get the stuffed animals?"

My long-term goal isn't to manipulate behavior by making life unpleasant with external demands until he complies. That's not mentoring, that's policing.

There are several goals in this example. One goal is to develop a culture in the home where we all work together. Not because it's a rule that we do so. Not because there will be punishments if someone doesn't. But because parents have set an example of relating to them in that way since they were little. We're a team. We help each other. If someone is tired and needs help, of course we help them. If furniture needs to be moved, and you're a strong teenager who can move furniture more easily than your mom, of course you'll help her. If someone left a mess, of course you'll help clean it up, especially if you're much more bothered by the mess than they are, and especially if you're an adult who doesn't see a mess as overwhelming as a six-year-old might. If you grow up in an atmosphere where people help each other, chances are you'll grow up to be someone who does just that.

The challenge is that most of us grew up in a culture that treats work as an undesirable hardship, so we need to learn to suck it up and get it done. Most of us were forced to do things during our entire childhoods. When you see kids in school who wait until the night before to finish a big assignment, usually it's something that has no meaning to them beyond the need to get a good grade. They dread it, they resent it, and might even feel bad about themselves because they've been told they shouldn't resent it. When kids are given the freedom to choose their own lives and do work that is meaningful to them, there is no need to worry that they won't do what they need to do to meet their individual goals.

Changing our attitudes about work requires us to mindfully think through whether we want to do each thing and why. It leaves us only doing work that we have chosen to do for a reason that is meaningful to us, and that enables us to work with more joy. It's not an easy shift to make, but if we work on it, healing will happen through generations.

Another goal in the example is to have the environment you live in neat and clean. That's not my strong point, since I tend to not pay attention to or notice visual things. I'm the type of person who will come home to my husband having cleaned the house or painted the walls and not notice that it's any different. So, while individual preferences about neatness come into play, it's important to at least have kids grow up knowing that if they leave crumbs all over the floor, ants might move in. And if enough toys are on the floor, someone might trip over them and get hurt. At six, they might not realize how important it is to keep a house bug-free. As they get older, though, they will— even if no one ever punished them for not cleaning up when they were six.

My friend protested. This was so different from how she had raised her kids, and it was hard for her to grasp. "But your kids could have turned out to just expect to be waited on hand and foot, and not ever help at all because they know you'll just do it."

No, because I am my kids' partner. We haven't created a culture of anyone being waited on hand and foot, or anyone being a martyr. We have created a culture of everyone keeping each other's needs in mind, and everyone helping cheerfully when others need it. We've done that by the older people setting the example for the younger people. We haven't done it by using coercion, because coercion would work against the goal of creating willing, mindful helpfulness.

"You shouldn't be their partner, you should be their parent," she said. "Their peers are their partners."

I'm not the same kind of partner as the kid who plays tag with them at the playground. I'm their partner who's an adult with the goal of helping them pursue their dreams and develop their interests. I'm the partner who is also their parent, who has earned their respect by respecting them.

Since this is so different than how we grew up, it takes some relearning of old thought patterns. Let me tell you, it's a huge growth process to try having a good attitude about doing dishes then, on top of that, have a small child want to help. And by help, I mean take four times as long to get the job done and require you to get many towels to clean up the spilled water on the floor. And maybe not have time to make anything more than peanut butter and jelly for dinner because cleaning the dishes was more of an all-afternoon learning activity than a quick chore. The long-term benefits make it worth it.

My son is taller than me, so he took down a box on a top shelf for me. He doesn't like to bake, so I made him the cookies he was hungry for. He doesn't snap his fingers and say, "Woman! In the kitchen!" And I don't demand that he stop playing his video game right now to get something on the top shelf for me. But if I know there's a craving, I think about my schedule and see if there's a way to gift him with cookies. And if he's walking past, or at a place in his game that is easy to pause, it only takes him a few seconds to reach something high for me.

It's a kind of family values that we've passed on to our kids through example. They're values that are ingrained pretty deeply now that they're older. And on top of those values is a type of flow. A mindfulness in how we live and interact. No one is forced to serve others, but we are happier, more peaceful, and even more productive in the pursuits of our individual goals when we actively show love and support to those who are on the same family team.

Chapter Eight

The Real World

Sometimes grandparents are concerned that their unschooled grandchildren have so much freedom that when they grow up, they won't be able to cope with the real world.

However, in the real world we have the freedom to choose among many different lifestyles and make a living in many different ways. In school, kids don't get nearly as many choices as they would in the real world. Unschoolers aren't in school preparing for the real world, they're already in it. They have spent their entire childhoods in partnership with their parents, doing what it takes to meet their goals.

Dealing With Mean or Difficult People

"They need school so they learn to deal with bullies" is a concern unschoolers often hear.

The stereotypical bully is the big kid who beats up smaller kids and steals their lunch money. In the real world, if someone tried to threaten me into giving them money, I'd call the police. If I were walking or taking public transportation along a familiar route and found it to be unsafe because of bullies, I wouldn't go that route anymore.

School kids often don't have the power to remove themselves from a situation. They're told they have to go to school and ride the bus or be in a program where the bullies are. They are sometimes told to "play nice with their friends" when they complain, as though everyone their age is automatically their friend, and if they would just be nice and sweet, all the problems would be solved.

Unschooled kids don't have to stay in a situation they don't want to be in, so they don't become adults who think they have to stay in a situation where they are treated poorly. They have always been allowed to speak their minds, so they're less likely to cower and be intimidated.

When she was a young teen, my daughter was interested in a basketball program held at a local school. The coach yelled, threatened, and was generally rude to the kids during the introduction meeting. We both looked around the room, wondering why any of those kids would choose to put themselves under the instruction of a coach who didn't treat young athletes with respect. I don't know how many of those kids went on to sign up for the program, but my daughter didn't. She knew that if she did, she'd be willingly putting herself under the authority of someone who was a bully. As an adult, she doesn't associate with mean people either. She doesn't choose to work for a mean boss, stay in relationships with mean men, or join an organization where the people are mean and unhelpful.

College and Living Lives
We Can Be Proud Of

If an unschooled kid has a desire for a career that requires a degree, college is the same as any other goal he has for himself: Research all the options he has and then pick the path that seems best for himself. Just as with anyone wanting to attend college, it might mean calling or meeting with a college admissions officer at the college he'd like to attend for advice on how to prepare. For some unschoolers, it might mean taking a course or two at a community college. Of course, it might mean that for someone who graduated from a traditional school, too. It might mean writing the first essay they've ever written. Colleges know that high school diplomas, transcripts, and experiences are different for kids who haven't been to school. Many colleges have a deep respect for that. If, instead of a traditional transcript, an unschooler can show the travels, hobbies, experiments, volunteer work, websites built, books read, and businesses started, he's likely to be smiled upon by admissions officers.

In her book *Homeschooling Our Children, Unschooling Ourselves*, author Allison McKee describes her son's science learning on his high school transcript that was created for college admission. He had a passion for fly fishing, which covered "entomology, ichthyology, river and lake ecology, physics, and a category we simply called 'miscellaneous.' Under each of these headings we listed the books and videos Christian had used as resources. In all we listed over thirty books (none of them traditional textbooks) with titles like *The Trout and the Fly*, by Clark and Goddard; *Trout,* by Schweibert; *Tying Hatch Simulator Flies*, by Swischer and Richards; and *The Essence of Flycasting, Vols I, II,* by Krieger."

An unschooler who has developed his passions to the point where he has a sincere desire to pursue a career that requires a college degree is going to have material from life experiences to write an essay that an admissions officer should find pretty interesting.

Sandra Dodd is a long-time unschooler who maintains a very helpful website with lots of information about unschooling. On her page, Unschoolers in College, she quotes Pam Sorooshian, another long-time unschooler. "I have three unschooled kids now in their 20s. Today is my middle daughter's college graduation ceremony. She graduates with highest honors and as a member of Phi Beta Kappa (the most prestigious honor society). She has a double major—history and drama. She's going on to graduate school in the fall and plans to get a PhD. My oldest daughter just got her master's degree in counseling and works as a family therapist. My youngest daughter has an AA degree and a certificate in Interpreting for the Deaf and is a junior in college working on her Bachelor of Arts degree.

"Unschooling seemed to have given them HUGE advantages in college. They were, frankly, shocked at the poor preparation and attitudes of most other students. Other students seemed to them to be 'going through the motions,' but were not really interested in learning. It is hard to explain, but all three of my kids and all of their unschooled friends who have gone to college have repeatedly tried to articulate that there seemed to be 'something wrong' with so many of the other students and that they seemed actually resistant to learning. The unschooled kids were there because they wanted to be there, first of all. They knew they had a choice and that makes a big difference. A sense of coercion leads to either outright rebellion, passive resistance, or apathy and my kids saw all of those playing out among the majority of their fellow students.

"I have been a college professor for 36 years and have taught at community colleges and prestigious universities. VERY few students are there to learn— they are there to jump through the required hoops to get the degree. The unschooled kids (I've had a few in my classes) far outshine most of the other students. Even unschooled kids I didn't think of as academic-leaning kids have done extremely well in college if they decided to go for their own reasons." http://sandradodd.com/college

In a recent survey of grown unschoolers by Harvard researcher Peter Gray, 75% of those who had always been unschooled had some form of higher education and 58% had at least a bachelor's degree or were working on one. To compare that to the general population, the United States Bureau of Labor Statistics reports that "In October 2015, 69.2% of 2015 high school graduates were enrolled in colleges or universities."

www.psychologytoday.com/blog/freedom-learn/201406/survey-grown-unschoolers-i-overview-findings

www.bls.gov/news.release/hsgec.nr0.htm

There are also many who follow creative pursuits, such as writers, artists, musicians, and photographers. Some are full-time parents. In Gray's survey, 48% of those surveyed were pursuing creative arts. Of those who always had been unschooled (as opposed to those who had only been unschooled for part of their childhood), 79% were pursuing careers in the creative arts.

Another interesting statistic of grown unschoolers from his survey is that 53% of the respondents were entrepreneurs, and of those in the always-unschooled group, 63% were. That's a very high number compared to the general population. According to an October 22, 2015, article entitled "Three-in-Ten U.S. Jobs Are Held by the Self-Employed and the Workers They Hire," the self-employed, 14.6 million in all, represented 10% of the nation's 146 million workers."

www.pewsocialtrends.org/2015/10/22/three-in-ten-u-s-jobs-are-held-by-the-self-employed-and-the-workers-they-hire/

If they aren't forced to go to school and do home-work, how will they get up and go to a job they hate and do mindless work just because the boss says to? Chances are they won't. Of the grown unschoolers in Gray's survey, 77% said there was a clear relationship between their adult employment and their childhood interests. They'll be their own boss, doing work they enjoy, and while they certainly will be able to get themselves out of bed to do what needs to be done (anyone who has ever worked for herself knows that successful entrepreneurship requires many hours and hard work), they'll be doing it because they have a real reason that is meaningful to them.

Unschooling produces a high number of people in business for themselves, often doing highly creative things. They enjoy their work, contribute to society in meaningful ways, and pay their bills. They are competent, literate, interesting adults.

Many Paths to Choose From

One of the strengths of unschooling is that there are many choices available to the unschooler from the time she's a baby. A person who is raised this way is used to finding creative means to meet their goals.

I overheard a grandmother at the store bragging about her grandson, who was attending an impressive university, doing impressive-sounding things. "We're really proud of him," she said.

I'm glad she's proud of him. Studying at a university is a fine thing to do. But if he hadn't gone to an impressive university to do impressive-sounding things, would she still be proud? I hope so.

I read a message board once where people were discussing what unschooled kids do when they grow up, and someone mentioned a grown unschooler they knew who "only worked on a farm." Critics said they wanted more for their kids than farm work.

What I want for my children is for them to know themselves so well that they know exactly what their hearts yearn for and they do what it takes to make it happen. If farming accomplishes that for them, good. If a college degree accomplishes that for them, good. If art does that for them, good. Whatever it is that does that for them is what I want for them.

My daughter completed one semester at college. When she realized how much debt that first semester created, she decided not to continue. She had gotten all A's, so the school called her to ask why she wasn't continuing. She told them that if she continued with her college degree, she would have to work to pay off her debt. She wanted to unschool her kids, not send them to school because she had to get a job to pay back her student loans. She said no to college and instead started an online business that not only supports her children but allowed her dad to retire early.

While the doors of universities swing open just as widely for unschoolers as they do for anyone else, college isn't a more respectable choice. We shouldn't push them into college just because we want to say, "My granddaughter is a surgeon." Or "My grandson is getting his master's degree." What they choose should be about them, not us.

I also have wondered at the idea of expecting eighteen year olds to know what they want to do for the rest of their lives and to commit many years and dollars toward a degree for a career that might not interest them in ten years. How many adults wish they could escape the daily grind but don't because it would be a waste of their college education to not work in that field? The important thing is that a young person knows herself so well that, while she might not know what she wants to do for the rest of her life, she knows what she would like to do next and considers college as only one of many possible paths to her goal. Unschoolers have spent their childhoods knowing if none of the paths in front of them take them where they want to go, or if none of the paths seem like an enjoyable journey, they can create their own path. It's no different when making choices about lifestyle and how they'll earn money to support that lifestyle. Sure, how they'll afford to feed and house themselves is a part of the puzzle that they have to figure out, but it's only a part of the puzzle. Unless they want them to be, their title and career don't have to be the primary focus of their lives.

One of my sons was a Boy Scout for a while. In Cub Scouts, he had earned every possible sports and academic award pin. He said he wanted to earn every badge he possibly could for Boy Scouts, too, and started off working very hard at it. His goal was something that very few boys ever accomplish, so it would be a big deal in the Boy Scout world. After a few years, he stopped. "If I'm going to do those things," he said, "I'll do them because I want to. Not because I get a badge for doing them." I respect when my kids want to try new things as well as when they want to stop pursuing something.

But I had this niggling disappointment. As I examined why I was disappointed, I realized it was because my kid was working toward doing something that was brag-worthy in the mainstream world that cared about awards, degrees, and certificates. I could hold it up to all the people who doubted unschooling and say, "See how well unschooling works! I didn't make him do it, and look what he accomplished!"

There must have been a remnant of mainstream schoolish thinking inside me that yearned for my son to keep doing something that was no longer important to him. In spite of how much I've studied about learning, child development, and unschooling philosophy, I wanted to look good to a society that revered school. Just a remnant, though. I'm proud that he values his time and analyzes his desires so much that he chose to not continue to participate in an activity that no longer held meaning for him.

At this time, none of my children are interested in college. My youngest is only seventeen, and doesn't have any big future plans. That's okay with me. Just as I didn't worry if he learned to walk or read according to an arbitrary schedule, I don't worry now. One of the benefits of unschooling is that kids can take as long as they need to think through ideas and plans. I admit that a part of me wouldn't mind bragging about deans' lists and top honors. That pride doesn't have anything to do with what is actually best for my children. We say that we just want our kids to be happy. And somewhere in our purely intellectual and philosophical reasoning, as well as deep inside our hearts when we're able to be transparently honest with ourselves, we know it's true. We want our children and grandchildren to find work, play, and love that fulfills them and fills them with joy and purpose. Society tells us other things are important, too, though, and sometimes the voices of our hearts and society conflict.

Finding Work

My husband worked for twenty-two years in a job he hated. He had been raised with the mindset that responsible people faithfully go to school or work. Only after you've put in your time do you get to enjoy whatever part of your day you have left, if you have any time left after preparing dinner and doing household chores. Many of us did not learn as kids to discover who we are and explore our passions. We didn't learn—really learn to the point where we had practiced doing it and it became second nature—that it's okay to choose the way we live.

My grandson took karate for a few months. He liked it in the beginning, but soon lost interest. When my daughter told the karate instructor that her son wanted to take a break, the instructor said that she shouldn't let him quit because, when he grows up, he'll think it's okay to quit his job.

When I heard this story, I said, "But it is okay for him to quit his job!" There are ways to support yourself that don't require you to stick at something you don't like. It took my husband until he was forty-five years old to realize that he could quit. He retired early because he didn't want to spend any more years doing something he hated in exchange for a paycheck. There are other ways to support himself and his family. He learned that he loves working at our daughter's online business.

One way to have the time and energy to do more of what you love is to say no to what you don't love. Many adults don't know how to do this because as kids, they were told that they had to do everything they were told. Saying no is a lesson that I'm learning as an adult. The need to please my teachers and parents was so ingrained into me as a child that I still sometimes feel guilty when I say no to something that isn't right for me. I don't want my kids to feel that guilt.

Of course, sometimes you have to do things you don't want to do in life. Or at least you have to do things if you want your life to look a certain way. Not everyone has the same goals for how they want their lives to look, and that's okay. Some people are willing to work long hours for a more expensive house, and some are satisfied with a small, simple shelter in the woods or even living full time in an RV. Some people want a five-bedroom home, and some are okay sharing expenses with several roommates. Whatever a person needs to feel satisfied with his life is what he needs to earn money for.

In Chapter Two, I talked about how times are changing. It used to be that you worked hard at a job, were loyal to your boss and your company, and were comfortable believing you would keep the same job until you retired. That's not how it is anymore, even for people who follow all the mainstream rules. We've all heard of college graduates working at fast food restaurants because they can't get a job in the fields they studied.

What I want for my kids and grandkids isn't to automatically follow the formula of school-college-job-mortgage-retirement that society still pushes onto young people. Rather, I want them to really think about what they want out of life. Only once they know themselves well and have thoroughly thought through their dreams and goals can they make a decision about the steps to take to make those dreams and goals come true. Those steps might include a college degree or a mainstream job, house, and lifestyle, or it may not.

Some unschooling families look pretty much the same as their neighbors except that their kids don't go to school. Others find ways to afford the unschooling lifestyle in unconventional ways. Some families thrive with homesteading: growing their own food, raising their own animals, making their own clothes, and creating art from their home. Some trade their mortgage for an RV and travel full time. Some have family businesses that allow all the adults to work from home, often including the children in their work.

One of the biggest things my heart is drawn to is helping unschoolers. I'm working on business possibilities that will help people learn about unschooling, help people unschool better, and connect unschoolers with other unschoolers. Those are all things I can do from a computer whether I'm at home, in the car, or at a café wherever I'm visiting.

Thanks to today's technology, we can run Internet-based businesses not just from our homes, but in our cars and in coffee shops anywhere. My daughter and I often take turns driving while the other sits in the passenger seat with a laptop getting work done. Years ago, people had to be in an office to respond to clients' questions and concerns. Now we can see a notification on our iPhones and answer a question while our kids enjoy the playground. Technology has unchained us from our desks.

Technology has also expanded our potential customer base. If we knit scarves, make soap, write books, produce videos, or make toys, we can sell those things on a variety of online marketing sites. When I was planning a children's craft for a homeschool group that involved gluing cutout trees, I was short on time so I ordered precut trees from an online seller who owns a die-cut machine. If you don't think your unschooled young person is earning a living, are you sure? Maybe she's selling paper trees on Etsy. My daughter makes money by buying wholesale products that she can sell on Amazon. We have encountered people who thought she didn't work at all because she orders her products while on the road to adventures with her kids.

We can specialize in things of particular interest to us because of the Internet as well. Our accountant specializes in the particular sales tax needs of Amazon sellers. He might not have enough customers if he only puts up a shop in his hometown, but he certainly does through his online business. Likewise, consultants and counselors who specialize in a narrow niche can find customers online that they might not find in their hometown.

If a grown unschooler wants a traditional job that requires a high school diploma, that's not a problem. Unschooling parents can issue homeschool diplomas for their kids.

Training for one job doesn't mean you have to stay in that job forever. You can work as an auto mechanic for years and then decide you want to be an attorney. And an attorney can quit practicing law to work on cars. Happiness and fulfillment are the important things.

We all have choices. Unschooling doesn't take choices away, it expands the choices.

Chapter Nine

Healing a Fractured Relationship

If your relationship with your adult children or grandchildren is fractured, your best bet for healing it is to state with respect, honesty, and humility your intention to mend your relationship. Building relationships with their children is a key focus of unschooling parents, so they'll likely respect your desire to build a better relationship with them. Even if they were the ones to draw back from the relationship, I recommend telling them that even though you have had some reservations about the unschooling lifestyle, you respect that they're doing it. Then tell them flat out that you love them and want to be more involved and get to know your grandchildren better.

There are times that we forget to tell the people we care about the most basic, important things, like that we love them and want to spend quality time with them. Maybe because those feelings are a deep part of who we are, and we assume they know it. People have insecurities and doubts all the time, though, and these are the kinds of things that we just have to come right out and say sometimes.

I know it's scary and risky because you're putting yourself out there, making yourself vulnerable to rejection. To be rejected by your children, especially when you're so honest and open, is one of the worst rejections of all. But this is important, and definitely worth the risk. Some very sensitive people will take a longer time than others to start trusting. Just continue being patient and understanding, and hopefully they'll come around.

There are times when unschoolers withdraw themselves and their children, either physically or emotionally, from their parents and relatives because they worry about some type of threat. Either they're worried that you'll discipline differently (put the kids in time-out or threaten to spank them, which unschoolers definitely don't do), bribe the kids to get them to do things your way, speak to their children disrespectfully, report them to children's social services, or make them or their children feel bad about themselves. If that's the case, be gently persistent yet patient as you wait to earn their trust.

"I'm sorry" can go a long, long way, even if they overreacted about something and it's not all your fault. Because even though it sounds all trite and sappy to say that we're older and wiser, it really is true. We know, when we're really honest, that the desired results are more important than our pride.

Tell them that you know you've had issues in the past, but you've read this book and you really want to make things right with them. Unschooling is a huge paradigm shift, and no matter how well you think you understand unschooling, you might find yourself doing something that doesn't fit with unschooling philosophy. Ask them to gently tell you if you do something to offend. That way, hopefully they won't automatically shut you out again. And if they do come to you, try not to get defensive. Model for them how to create good relationships. Be very clear that you're not a threat to them or their lifestyle.

Of course, words without actions are meaningless. Back up your words with offers to get involved in supportive ways. I'll cover ideas in the next chapter.

There's no guarantee, of course. Relationships are difficult and everyone has a different history. But while your chances of getting them to change or see the need for schoolwork or stricter rules are practically zero, your chances of being involved in a healthy relationship with them after you've let go of the need to change them is pretty good.

If you're the one who has withdrawn yourself from time spent with them, please know that it's likely that they really, really would value your involvement, as long as the involvement respects that they're unschoolers.

Chapter Ten

Grandma, We Need You!

If, for some reason, your unschooling family hasn't told you, I will tell you on their behalf: Grandma, we need you.

When my children were born, I resolved to be the best mom that I could possibly be. I was there when my grandkids were born, and as I held each of them for the first time, I resolved to be the best grandma I could be. I want to be their rock. I want my grandkids to know that no matter what happens in life, they can come to Gram, and Gram will have their back.

As anyone who has witnessed a birth knows, it's not just a baby who is born. New parents are born as well. Having a baby changes you. As I looked at my daughter's face and saw the pride, joy, and absolute bliss at the birth of her babies, I renewed my resolve that I had made so many years ago when she was born. This time, I resolved to be the best parent of an adult child that I could be.

When I was a child, I was told that when my grandmother had babies, she and her newborn stayed in bed for ten days. For ten days, her sisters and mother did her family's laundry, cooked meals for her family, and took care of her other children. For ten days, she had nothing to do but sit in bed loving and feeding that baby.

I didn't appreciate that story until I had babies of my own. My second baby had colic. I remember a moment when he had been crying all night long and all morning long, and right before he finally fell asleep, he threw up all over the bathroom rug and all over my nightgown. I tiptoed to his crib and put him down in that careful way that we do when we don't want to wake a sleeping baby, then went to the bathroom to look at the rug that needed to be washed. I sat down on the bathroom floor and cried. I cried because I was so sleep-deprived. And the washing machine was down two flights of stairs, but I was still sore from having a baby and going down steps hurt. And my four-year-old wanted me to play Barbies with her, but I was just too exhausted, and I felt so guilty about that. And I had no idea what we were going to eat for dinner that night.

I wanted what my grandma had. There is such a gap between generations now. Way too much. We tell our kids, "Well, you're eighteen, and now you're on your own. Good luck."

People talk about how sad it is that we put our elderly in nursing homes and forget about them. It's sad to imagine a generation of people forgotten and discarded by the other generations.

But you know what else is sad?

A young mom who is exhausted and overwhelmed and doing it all on her own. A young dad who also was kept awake all night by the screaming baby, who had to get up and go to work anyway, then come home to make dinner and clean up before he collapsed into bed to get up and do it all over again the next day. A four-year-old who is still adjusting to having a new baby in the house, and no one will play with her.

Before they get so old that they can't take care of themselves anymore, Grandma and Grandpa can begin bridging the generation gap.

They can walk the crying baby while Mom finally takes a shower by herself then get the family something to eat and play Barbies for a while. They can provide company to a young mom who feels the need for adult conversation. They can pass on family lore through the stories of their childhood and stories passed on to them from their parents. As a matter of fact, they can spend so much time with the children that they became a natural part of their lives. As the kids get older, they might find themselves confiding in Grandma about problems and frustrations they face. And maybe she'll have advice. And maybe they'll take it because they've spent so much time with her that they've found her to be trustworthy.

Grandparent means a parent who is grand. A Grand Parent. That's a pretty important role. Involvement by grandparents and extended families is so good for kids, and is at a pretty weak level in our society. Many studies have shown the importance of a close relationship between grandparent and grandchild. For example, "A survey conducted by Oxford University and the Institute of Education in London found that children are generally happier if grandparents are involved in their upbringing."

www.grandparents.com/family-and-relationships/caring-for-children/study-grandparents-make-grandchildren-ha

Of course your involvement with your grandkids benefits them, but it benefits you, too. An August 12, 2013, article at cbsnews.com entitled "Good Grandparent, Grandchild Bond May Lower Depression Risk for Both" reports a study that shows that giving tangible support, such as rides to the store or financial assistance, benefits the grandparents' psychological health even more than it benefits the grandchildren's. Helping your grandchildren isn't just good for them, it's good for you.

www.cbsnews.com/news/good-grandparent-grandchild-bond-may-lower-depression-risk-for-both/

Unschooling parents don't want to be alienated from their parents, and they don't want their kids to be alienated from their grandparents. In fact, they often yearn for supportive involvement.

But it's also true that unschooling is their priority, so much so that if they feel their unschooling lifestyle is being attacked, sabotaged, or disrespected, they may pull away.

On behalf of the many unschooling parents who are hurt that their parents won't even try to understand unschooling, thank you for reading this book. Even if you don't fully agree with it, you cared about your relationship with them enough to try to understand. Because you care so much, you can go a long way in healing the generational disconnect that is so prevalent in our society.

My heart is with my children and my children's children. I want to spend as much time as I can with them, and I want to make sure they know I'm interested in who they are and what they love. I want them to know without a doubt that I love them, not just because they're my kids and grandkids, but because I celebrate who they are as individuals.

At some point, I won't be here anymore. I want them to smile at their memories of me. On my deathbed, I won't care if I was able to go to my high school reunion and brag that my grandkids were on the honor roll. I will care if I'm a good memory for those to whom my memory really matters because I took the kids who were fascinated with sea creatures to the aquarium, helped them bake a birthday cake for their mom, and made foam pirate hats with them. Even when I don't understand their TV shows or their computer games, I make a point not to complain about them. I don't want to be remembered as a nagging grandma, always complaining about kids these days.

A student at a New York City university who had grown up in China told me that her home had no beauty products, and her mom was a staunch believer that wearing makeup or worrying about physical appearance was inexcusable vanity. Her mom even forbade her to pierce her ears because she believed men don't like that, and it would make her less marriageable.

The student said this is a common scenario in China. Now that she's on her own and choosing to wear makeup and a sophisticated hairstyle, she's worried about how the interaction with her mom will go when she sees her again.

When adult children turn away from their cultural and family traditions, it's often hard for their parents to accept. In many ways, radical unschoolers have turned away from mainstream culture. Not only do they go about education, discipline, and child-rearing in completely different ways, they also tend to look at things like careers and lifestyles in different ways. But we don't ever want our kids to be hesitant or worried about spending time with us or confiding in us. We know how much the generations of people need each other.

Please, get involved! Forced study and arbitrary rules won't work in your relationship with unschooled grandkids, but who you are as a person—your values and skill sets—will most certainly have an impact. It's said that people become like those they spend the most time with. Don't think that you won't have an influence on their character if you spend time simply enjoying being with them. And, of course, they'll have an influence on you as well.

It's always easiest to start with what you and your unschooling parents have in common, and here's what you both have in common: You both care about the children, want them to be happy, and want them to learn.

You might be itching to sit that little boy down and teach him phonics. Don't. You might want to quiz them to see if they know their times tables, but if you do, their mom will bare her fangs. You might want to hand the family a checklist of what schools say kids their age should know by now, but please know that won't go over well at all.

There are ways you can make a positive impact in their lives without stepping on any toes. You can even help them learn, although if you're only used to thinking of learning in terms of school-style learning, it might take some time to start recognizing natural learning.

A friend whose kids go to school told me that what I call unschooling, she calls life. I said, "Me, too!" If you're used to interacting with kids in the ways I describe, that's awesome. Successful unschooling requires us to lead enriching, interesting lives that we share with our children. Some people live those enriching, interesting lives with children and send them to school, so if you're one of those people, this will be easier for you. You just have to keep doing what you're doing (and maybe doing a little more of it, if you'd like) while letting go of school expectations.

If you go into this with an agenda to teach stuff you think they should know, they'll resent it. Even the kids will resent it. But, if you go into it with a desire to build a relationship with your grandchildren, they'll likely treasure your presence. In the next section, I'll give ideas for ways to get started interacting with your grandkids, but know that I do this with some hesitancy.

The reason I hesitate is that all kids are unique, and just because something is on my idea list doesn't mean that all kids will like it. Some activities that my kids loved are not things that my grandkids love.

These are only ideas, not a checklist. The minute a kid stops enjoying himself, or the minute things start flowing naturally to a different topic, or a different variation of the same topic, let it flow! Drop your agenda, or better yet, don't have an agenda at all. I know it's not always easy, even for me, and I've been unschooling for a lot of years. But if you determine to not be attached to any particular outcome, and to make a great relationships your priority, it will be enjoyable for everyone.

Ideas for Bonding With Your Unschooled Grandkids

1. Go for walks together

Walks to the end of town and back, through a busy city, on a nature trail, or on long, meandering country roads...it doesn't matter as long as both you and your grandchildren enjoy it. Walks sometimes lead to talking and meaningful conversation. It's a great way for you to learn more about each other.

If you see interesting things on the way, point them out. Are you good at identifying trees? Point out the different kinds, if they're interested. Stop to look at the centipede on a rock. If you know an interesting story about the guy who used to own a store you walk past, and you think they might be interested, tell the story.

If the kids play Pokémon GO®, help them find pokestops and gyms. If you don't understand the game, ask them about it!

In school terms, a walk might be considered phys ed or the conversation might be classified as science or social studies. But try not to think in those terms. If school had never been invented, would grandparents walk with their grandchildren, learning from each other? Absolutely. If the kids did go to school, would you worry about working social studies or science into your walk? Probably not. Just be Grandma, enjoying a walk with the grandkids.

On Earth Day, I took my grandkids and some garbage bags to a nature trail. We cleaned up garbage for a while, but then they saw water and wanted nothing more than to play in it. I sat in the grass, soaking up the sun, while they stirred the water with sticks, yelling, "Here, froggy, froggy." They didn't conjure any frogs, but they had a great time.

I didn't insist that they follow the agenda of collecting garbage just because that's what we had planned to do. I make sure I have extra clothes along so I don't have to worry if they get wet and dirty, and I've learned to give up on caring what others might think about a grandma sitting on the side of a trail while her grandkids play in puddles. I'm a writer, and I know that the best stories come from imaginative play. My *Cellular Spirits* series came about because of a game my kids played in the yard with shadows. Who knows where their play could lead us!

2. Make food together

It could be as simple as inviting them to make cookies with you. Yes, when you grab a one cup measure with the quick, natural explanation that it's all you need since you're doubling two half cups, they're learning fractions. But, please, don't turn making cookies into a lesson. Just be interested in them—what they think, feel, and wonder about.

And be interesting. Tell that story about when you were little and your grandmother made these cookies with you. Tell them about how the grocery store you had to run to for eggs was different when you were their age. Maybe you have a special family recipe handed down through the generations. Share it with them!

Unless they hate baking, or unless you hate baking. These are just suggestions, remember!

3. Share TV, movies, video games, and books

Or go to the movies. Watch stuff they're interested in, and make suggestions based on what you think they might like. Ask them questions if you don't understand something, and welcome their questions. Don't try to turn watching television into a lesson. If you really get in tune with the kids, you'll find the conversations flow naturally, just as they would with anyone you have a nice relationship with. Kids deserve authentic conversation and real answers to their questions. Not,

"Just because that's how we do it." All kids, whether they're unschooled or not, deserve to be answered by someone who makes them enough of a priority that they take their time to give a well thought out, honest, thorough answer.

Once, after an episode of *SpongeBob SquarePants®*, I pulled out a book that showed how to draw SpongeBob characters. If they hadn't liked it, I would have tossed it aside right away, but they got into it. They also asked about jellyfish after watching SpongeBob go fishing for jellyfish, so I Googled facts and images of jellyfish. We hung their drawings and their favorite jellyfish images all around the TV. It wasn't a school lesson, there were no tests and no boxes to check off that we covered topics in a science or art curriculum. It was simply a pleasant way for all of us to spend time together. Seek out things that might be interesting to them, while not taking it personally if you guessed wrong and they aren't interested after all.

Ask to borrow their books, even if it's one of those crazy Japanese manga books that you have to read backward or a book about a teenage vampire who sparkles.

If you sit down to watch them play video games, or even play with them, it's easier to understand the games. Lots of adults have their own Minecraft® accounts.

I played a video game with my teens once where a boss was trying to kill me, and I screamed the whole time. I mean, come on, he was trying to kill me! How could I not scream? They have the memory of their mom overreacting and being a horrible fighter in a video game, but they also laugh when they talk about it. I'm not a video game person, but I see what they're playing and respect that the games are important and valuable to them.

4. Share your hobbies

Woodworking, sewing, bird watching, fixing cars, skiing, or playing an instrument—whatever you enjoy, offer to do some of it with them. They might want to, or they might not.

It's always a shame to hear someone say, "Yeah, Grandma knew how to do that, but she never showed any of us." Pass on that knowledge—as much as they want to have it passed on to them.

Do you fish? They might like it. Or they might not. You never know until you ask.

Fishing is an opportunity for all kinds of biology learning, but don't try to turn it into a biology lesson. On the other hand, don't be afraid to talk about science if it comes up naturally, because science is part of life. Just fish, and the biology will happen on its own, as much as it needs to for that child on that day.

Fishing with grandkids might be an idyllic time of sitting on a bank, quietly enjoying each other's presence while waiting for the fish to bite. Or they might lose patience after ten minutes and want to skip rocks in the water. It's the time spent together that's important, not the activity.

5. Use whatever resources are unique to you

Are there cool construction vehicles digging up a road near your house? Maybe they'd like to watch them. Does your job give you special access to something your grandkids might like?

A local homeschooler invited a homeschool group to her dad's cabin in the woods to catch tadpoles and salamanders in a vernal pool. My daughter and I drove together and tag teamed keeping an eye on the kids. There was *oohing* and *aahing* as they caught and observed the critters we pulled from the pond, followed by friendly sword fights among little boys. That grandfather opening up his property to a homeschool group benefited more than his own grandchildren.

6. Scope out cool new places.

Playgrounds, zoos, children's museums, libraries, art museums, science museums, community pro-grams...there are tons of resources out there if you look for them. Pick up the "What's Happening in Our Community" brochures in your town and surrounding areas. Read bulletin boards.

I regularly watch unschool and homeschool groups for activities the grandkids would love. Even though we're unschoolers and not homeschoolers, homeschool groups often have some really cool activities that don't conflict with unschooling philosophy. Other community and online groups have activities your grandkids might be interested in as well. We regularly check an online kids' hiking group for activities that my grandkids might enjoy.

Is there a new horseback riding opportunity that your horse-crazy granddaughter might enjoy? A train ride for the train-obsessed toddler?

Explore and discover together. That they are engaged and enjoying themselves is more important than what the activity actually is. In his book *How Children Learn*, John Holt says, "What teachers and learners need to know is what we have known for some time: First, that vivid, vital, pleasurable experiences are the easiest to remember, and secondly, that memory works best when unforced, that it is not a mule that can be made to walk by beating it."

Check out memberships and reciprocal memberships. Reciprocal membership info can usually be found on the organization's website. Many zoos, science centers, and children's museums offer free or half-price admission to other zoos, science centers, and children's museums. My daughter and I live in the same house, so for memberships that allow any two adults in the same household to be named, my daughter and I can both use the same membership. Other memberships allow grandparents to be on the membership for a slightly higher price. Memberships make great gifts, too!

Since my grandkids love to travel, we use the reciprocal feature of memberships pretty heavily. With our membership to the Whitaker Science Center in Harrisburg, we were able to get into the Academy of Natural Science Museum in Philadelphia and the

Children's Museum of Pittsburgh for free. Our zoo membership gets us into the zoo for free, as well as half price at other zoos.

Go as slowly or as quickly as the kids want to. If they want to spend an hour at the zoo playground and it will mean they won't get to see all the animals, that's okay. Take them again some other time.

We go to multiple playgrounds in different cities. If your town or city has a great playground that they love, wonderful! But if they're bored with the same old playground, scope out new, interesting playgrounds in other towns. Sometimes my daughter has an appointment in a town that has an awesome playground. Instead of watching her kids at home, I go along and she drops us off at the playground. The neat thing about this playground is that it always has kids to play with. Sometimes we go to playgrounds where you wonder where all the kids are. Not this one! The culture of play is strong there, and more often than not, we run into other families that parent in ways that are compatible with our unschooling lifestyle. Occasionally, we run into adults yelling at kids not to climb up the slide or not to take their shoes off or not to get too dirty, but it's rare. If you can find a good playground that the kids love, it's worth driving out of the way. Pack a picnic lunch, or plan a dinner out at a restaurant near the playground. Take a book for yourself, in case they get into playing and don't need you, but also be prepared to never open the book if your involvement is required. If they want to play with you the whole time, play!

I've often given the advice to young mothers that, "The days are long, but the years are short." I recently told my daughter, on the eve of my son's nineteenth birthday, that one day her little boy will be nineteen years old and not need to be at her side every moment of the day. I'm beginning to suspect it might even be truer for grandkids. We're making plans for my oldest grandchild's fifth birthday, and I don't know where those past five years have gone. Time seems to be going faster nowadays. As long as my health allows it, and as long as they want me to, I'll play.

Libraries are another community resource that can be easy to overlook, especially for people who remember the days when libraries were somber places where you never dared to make a peep or the librarian would angrily *shush* you. Many libraries now have games and toys available for kids to play with, computers loaded with fun programs, and special activities. My grandson played his first game of Candy Land® at a library.

Last year we enjoyed a superhero-themed summer library program. There were superhero games, prizes, stories, and even free hot dogs and drinks. This year the theme is sports, and the grandkids are excited about going to a kung fu demonstration.

Libraries aren't just about borrowing books anymore. You can borrow DVDs, music, and computer games as well. Some libraries even loan passes to museums.

You can visit libraries in different towns. Each one is unique and has different things to offer. Call ahead and ask what you need to access materials from that library as an out-of-town resident. Many states let you get a library card in other libraries for free if you have a card from your home library.

7. Mess around

Exciting trips and playing at science museums are great memory makers, but so are the little things that can be done on a lazy afternoon. Show them how to draw a cube, play tic-tac-toe, or whistle with a blade of grass. It doesn't have to be a big, expensive day out in order to be meaningful.

8. What do they want to do?

Ask them! They might want to do something you never would have thought of.

9. Don't forget the adults!

The adults could benefit from your involvement as well. All parents get tired and overwhelmed and need a break sometimes. Sometimes they just want adult company, and sometimes they want an hour or two off.

When you suggest things, make sure you tell the parents that they're welcome to come along or stay home, whatever would be most helpful to them. I go on lots of trips with my daughter and her kids, and that multigenerational bonding is a wonderful experience.

At different stages and ages in the kids' lives, differing needs might dictate how you can be most helpful. A breastfeeding mom might not want you to take her baby for the afternoon because pumping enough milk and dealing with full breasts would be more stressful than just keeping the baby with her. But, if you brought a home-cooked meal, keeping in mind everyone's tastes and eating restrictions (even if they're vegetarian or gluten free and you think that's ridiculous), it will likely be appreciated.

Communication is vital. It's always best to come right out and ask. "I found a movie I think the kids might like. Have they seen it? Do you think they might like it? Can I come watch it with them? I'll bring popcorn. Do you want to watch, too? Or would you prefer to have a date night with your husband? How can I help you? I want to be involved, and I want to do what is going to be the most helpful."

Adult children need more than your help. They, too, can benefit from your knowledge and companionship. If they're interested in gardening, and you know a lot about gardening, volunteer to spend an afternoon, or many afternoons, in the garden with them. Tell them those stories about things your mom used to say. Show that you're interested in them. Children love to feel important to their parents, no matter how old they are.

10. Money

Let's face it, one thing young parents often struggle with is money. Unschoolers might not need back-to-school shopping, uniforms, or school tuition, but the unschoolers I regularly interact with often say that money is a source of stress and they wish they were able to afford to do more awesome things with their kids. If you happen to be in a financial situation where you can afford it, buying family memberships to zoos, museums, amusement parks, funding trips, paying for gas, buying cool art supplies, games, and subscriptions are all things that unschooling families appreciate. If you're not sure what would help them most, ask!

Let It Flow

One night, I was reading bedtime stories to my grandkids while their mom took a bath. The next thing I knew, they were trying on shoes, most of which were several sizes too big for them. I put down the book to help the two-year-old put a snow boot on one foot and a flip-flop on the other. Trying on different combinations of shoes is what they wanted to do, so I followed their lead. I'm a writer and a book lover, so I had some internal resistance. How could trying on shoes possibly be more interesting than these beloved books? But I know that my interests aren't their interests, that I can't always recognize the learning that is certainly happening from every activity they choose, and that an evening of putting shoes over books won't hurt anything.

There's an art to unschooling that's enjoyable and even easy once you get into the rhythm of it. It's just finding that rhythm that can be hard initially. At the library one time with my grandkids, knowing that they liked the Pigeon Presents series of books by Mo Willems, I browsed the shelves for more Mo Willems books. I pulled out *Listen to My Trumpet!* and suggested it. If they weren't interested, that would have been fine, but they were. We took it home and read it, and they thought it was hilarious. I got the idea to get out my trombone and make sounds similar to those Piggie made in the book. They now ask me to play my trombone all the time, and they like to play it as well. That led me to getting out my clarinet and guitar.

One thing leads to another then another then another. It's like the picture book *If You Give a Mouse a Cookie*. You give him a cookie, and he'll want milk. He'll want a straw, then a napkin, then he'll look in the mirror to see if he has a milk moustache. While looking in the mirror, he'll realize he needs a trim, so he'll want scissors. It goes on as one thing leads to another then another. It's a silly children's story, but unschooling works the same way. You go to a restaurant with young children, and they wish they had their own restaurant, so you go home and make menus and cook a variety of simple foods and let them play waiter and take orders from the rest of the family for dinner. Helping them write words on the menu might look to some like a creative school project designed to encourage literacy, but to the unschooled child, it's just living life. If they really get into it, you could organize a tour of an actual restaurant or watch a TV show about owning a restaurant. I just let things unfold, insert a little bit of something interesting that I think might excite them, and see what happens.

If You Live Far Away

If you live a long distance from your grandkids, it's impossible to stop by with a movie and some popcorn or to take long afternoon walks with them. You can still become an important part of your grandkids' lives, though.

Every trip you make to visit (or every invitation you send them to visit) is well worth it. You have an opportunity to introduce them to an area other than the one where they live. I grew up living some distance from my grandparents, and I have very fond memories of the visits we took to be with them.

Thanks to technology, we can have great Skype® conversations with family who live far away. Kids often enjoy texting. You can send them frequent physical snail mail. Kids love to receive small gifts, notes, and postcards.

Many video games can be played long distance if both you and the grandkids have the same gaming systems. If the grandkids are interested, ask them for game suggestions. It could be a great bonding experience, well worth the effort to figure out the new technology.

Grandma, the Leader

You don't have to be authoritarian to be a good leader. In fact, the best leaders are also servants.

By serving your children and grandchildren, you also serve yourself. You provide yourself with a fulfilling, satisfying relationship with the people you love the most.

By becoming a regular, natural part of their lives, you'll get to relish the fact that these kids—the children of your children—won't have their childhoods pass with only seeing their grandparents on holidays. They'll remember peaceful, joyful relationships. There's so much they could learn from you, and just as important, there's so much you could learn from them.

Build the kind of relationship that if the rest of the family wants to take a vacation, but the thirteen-year-old really doesn't want to go and the parents are hesitant to let him home alone, he knows he's welcome to stay with you instead.

If someone is frustrating him or stressing him out, or the neighbor kid or the coach keeps picking on him, be a safe person for him to talk to.

Some people say, "That's great for your family because you do all kinds of interesting stuff with your kids. Not everyone does!" If your family is unschooling, they probably do things that their kids are interested in. But parents do get overwhelmed sometimes, no matter what their parenting philosophy. Life circumstances can keep them from doing as much as they'd like. So my challenge is, if you can let go of academic worries, even for only an afternoon at a time, go out and do interesting stuff with your grandkids. Just remember that they might not want to do all the things that you think they should want to do. If their best day imaginable is hanging out at the pool, take them to the pool. If their best day would be to have Grandma build track for their Thomas the Tank Engine™ trains, build track. If they love crafts and glue sticks, plan a craft. Be willing to abandon your craft plan and follow their lead if need be. Kids abandoning directions and doing it their own way is valuable, too. If you do interesting things with them, you'll be contributing to their learning, but you don't have to worry about that. Don't worry about anything other than you and your grandkids enjoying each other.

Be your grandkids' rock. Not the hard-nosed, make-them-do-as-they're-told kind of rock, but the kind of rock that is a stable source of all that is good and makes life worth living. Someone who is reliable, patient, joyful, and shows unconditional love and support. Someone who is older and wiser but doesn't lord it over them, who gives advice when it's asked for but sometimes just sits and listens. Someone who offers plenty of hugs when needed, and from whom they don't have to fear punishment or harsh words. Having a grandparent like that can make a world of difference in a child's life. And having grandchildren who are loved and supported like that can make a world of difference in a grandparent's life.

If you would like to read more of my writing about unschooling, visit my blog at:

www.sheilabaranoski.com/

Made in the USA
Middletown, DE
05 July 2017